WITHDRAWN

CIVIL LIBERTIES
THE FIGHT FOR PERSONAL FREEDOM

By Allison Krumsiek

Portions of this book originally appeared in *Civil Liberties* by Leanne Currie-McGhee.

LUCENT
PRESS

Published in 2018 by
Lucent Press, an Imprint of Greenhaven Publishing, LLC
353 3rd Avenue
Suite 255
New York, NY 10010

Copyright © 2018 Greenhaven Press, a part of Gale, Cengage Learning
Gale and Greenhaven Press are registered trademarks used herein under license.

All new materials copyright © 2018 Lucent Press, an Imprint of Greenhaven Publishing, LLC.

All rights reserved. No part of this book may be reproduced in any form without permission
in writing from the publisher, except by a reviewer.

Designer: Seth Hughes
Editor: Jennifer Lombardo

Cataloging-in-Publication Data

Names: Krumsiek, Allison.
Title: Civil liberties: the fight for personal freedom / Allison Krumsiek.
Description: New York : Lucent Press, 2018. | Series: Hot topics | Includes index.
Identifiers: ISBN 9781534561458 (library bound) | ISBN 9781534561465 (ebook)
Subjects: LCSH: Civil rights–United States–Juvenile literature.
Classification: LCC KF4750.K78 2018 | DDC 342.7308'5–dc23

Printed in the United States of America

CPSIA compliance information: Batch #BS17KL: For further information contact Greenhaven Publishing LLC, New York, New
York at 1-844-317-7404.

Please visit our website, www.greenhavenpublishing.com. For a free color catalog of all our
high-quality books, call toll free 1-844-317-7404 or fax 1-844-317-7405.

CONTENTS

Adolescence is a time when many people begin to take notice of the world around them. News channels, blogs, and talk radio shows are constantly promoting one view or another; very few are unbiased. Young people also hear conflicting information from parents, friends, teachers, and acquaintances. Often, they will hear only one side of an issue or be given flawed information. People who are trying to support a particular viewpoint may cite inaccurate facts and statistics on their blogs, and news programs present many conflicting views of important issues in our society. In a world where it seems everyone has a platform to share their thoughts, it can be difficult to find unbiased, accurate information about important issues.

It is not only facts that are important. In blog posts, in comments on online videos, and on talk shows, people will share opinions that are not necessarily true or false, but can still have a strong impact. For example, many young people struggle with their body image. Seeing or hearing negative comments about particular body types online can have a huge effect on the way someone views himself or herself and may lead to depression and anxiety. Although it is important not to keep information hidden from young people under the guise of protecting them, it is equally important to offer encouragement on issues that affect their mental health.

The titles in the Hot Topics series provide readers with different viewpoints on important issues in today's society. Many of these issues, such as teen pregnancy and Internet safety, are of immediate concern to young people. This series aims to give readers factual context on these crucial topics in a way that lets them form their own opinions. The facts presented throughout also serve to empower readers to help themselves or support people they know who are struggling with many of the challenges adolescents face today. Although negative viewpoints are not ignored or downplayed, this series allows young people to see that the challenges they face are not insurmountable. Eating disorders can be overcome, the Internet can be navigated safely, and pregnant teens do not have to feel hopeless.

Quotes encompassing all viewpoints are presented and cited so readers can trace them back to their original source, verifying for themselves whether the information comes from a reputable place. Additional books and websites are listed, giving readers a starting point from which to continue their own research. Chapter questions encourage discussion, allowing young people to hear and understand their classmates' points of view as they further solidify their own. Full-color photographs and enlightening charts provide a deeper understanding of the topics at hand. All of these features augment the informative text, helping young people understand the world they live in and formulate their own opinions concerning the best way they can improve it.

Understanding Civil Liberties

Throughout history, people have fought to protect their freedom. Sometimes these fights are violent, such as when a government is overthrown by the people. Other times the fights are more peaceful, such as when people circulate petitions and organize protest marches. However, whether peaceful or violent, the aim is the same: to protect basic human rights.

The belief that people are born with certain freedoms is part of a philosophy of natural rights. Philosopher John Locke wrote about this theory in the 17th century. In 1689, Locke published the *Two Treatises of Government*. He wrote that all people are born with natural rights, such as the right to life, liberty, and property. He believed that a government had no right to take these away. If a government tried to take away people's freedoms, Locke believed the people should rebel against the government.

In 1776, the American colonists rebelled against the British government because the colonists felt England was violating their civil liberties.

Liberties' Historic Beginnings

Civil liberties are natural rights that are free from government interference. Common civil liberties are the freedom of religion, the freedom of speech, the right to a fair trial, and the right to privacy. Governments that support civil liberties make laws to protect them.

The Magna Carta was one of the first documents to protect people's civil liberties. It was a document issued in AD 1215 that forced the king of England to respect certain rights of his subjects. Even as king, he could not interfere with these rights. One of the rights was habeas corpus, which allowed the king's subjects to appeal against unlawful imprisonment.

Although the Magna Carta protected some freedoms, it did not safeguard religious freedom. Puritans and other religious groups could not worship the way they wanted in England. During the 1600s, many of them left England. They went to America and started the first British colonies there, taking the concept of civil liberties with them.

The creation of the Magna Carta showed that even kings are expected to respect the rights of their subjects.

Exercising Civil Liberties

When the British colonies in America broke free of Great Britain, the Founding Fathers formed a central government, but they structured it so that the government could not violate people's natural rights. They adopted the Bill of Rights, which specifically states which liberties the government will not violate.

Since that time, civil liberties have remained a core value of the United States. Although there have been violations of civil liberties, people's freedoms have ultimately been upheld. People in the United States can practice their religions, say what they believe, and make their own personal decisions.

Protests are prime examples of people exercising their civil liberties in the United States. People are free to protest the government's actions as long as they follow certain laws, such as getting a permit and not trespassing. If they follow the rules, people have the right to make speeches, chant, and display signs protesting the government's actions. For example, over the course of nine days in April 2016, protesters marched from Philadelphia, Pennsylvania, to the White House in Washington, D.C., to protest the influence of money in politics.

Civil Liberties Are Not Guaranteed

Republics or democracies that guarantee civil liberties, such as the United States, have a constitution or a bill of rights that protects citizens. However, not all countries protect civil liberties. Authoritarian countries typically do not protect civil liberties. Leaders of these countries believe that free speech and other freedoms can cause problems.

In wartime, governments often neglect the civil liberties of the people they represent. In Syria, President Basshar Al-Assad has been involved in a civil war since 2005. Al-Assad has been accused of committing human rights violations against people who speak out against his government. Activists against the war inside Syria are often held illegally in state prisons. Many of these activists are abused by police and jailers.

Other countries claim to guarantee civil rights but do not actually protect them. China's constitution guarantees civil liberties for Chinese citizens, but the government suppresses opposition to its policies. People who speak out against the Chinese government can be arrested and charged with subversion. According to the Committee to Protect Journalists, the crackdown on free speech has escalated since President Xi Jinping took office in 2013. As of 2015, there are 49 known journalists held in Chinese prisons for speaking against the government.

Issues in the Court System

Even in countries that protect civil liberties, there are controversies. Sometimes a person's right to free speech may infringe on another person's right to privacy. Other times, national security issues may override a person's right to privacy. People take these issues to court for resolution. The court's role is to interpret laws that either protect civil liberties or override them.

Many civil liberties matters are handled by the U.S. federal court system. A federal district court will first hear the case. District courts have jurisdiction to hear nearly all categories of federal cases, including both civil and criminal matters. A person can appeal the ruling from a district court. If an appeal is allowed, a federal court of appeals may hear it next. An appeal from this court can go to the U.S. Supreme Court.

Some civil liberties cases are handled by the state court system, which is separate from the federal system. A state case begins with a local trial court and may then be appealed to a state appeals court. This may also be appealed to the highest court in the state, called a state supreme court in some states and a court of appeals in others. For example, the Washington State Supreme Court heard a privacy case in 2008. The Wahkiakum School District had a policy that its schools could test any student for drugs, even if the student was not suspected of using illegal drugs. The American Civil Liberties Union (ACLU), which represented two families of students in the Wahkiakum School District, took the school district to court over the issue. The ACLU said the drug tests violated the students' right to privacy. The Washington Supreme Court ruled that officials should not violate individual privacy when there is no reason to believe that a student has used illegal drugs.

The highest court in the United States is the U.S. Supreme Court. Cases heard in this court set precedents for the entire country. The Supreme Court consists of the chief justice and associate justices. The Supreme Court hears some cases that began in the federal or state courts and were appealed. It chooses cases that concern important questions about the Constitution or federal law.

In 2016, the Supreme Court heard a case involving a driver who refused an alcohol breath test after being pulled over by police and was arrested for his refusal. The case, *Missouri v. McNeely*, was filed by the ACLU on behalf of the driver. The question to the Supreme Court was whether it was lawful for the state to prosecute someone for refusing. Under the Fourth Amendment to the U.S. Constitution, "the right of the people to be secure in their persons, houses, papers, and effects, against unreasonable searches and seizures consent" is protected. The Supreme Court ruled that people have a right to refuse searches and breathalyzer tests if the police do not first obtain a warrant.

Complicated Civil Liberties

Over the years, U.S. courts have heard many cases about civil liberties, and the courts have decided whether laws have violated people's civil liberties. Today, there are many more civil liberties cases waiting to be heard on issues ranging from same-sex marriage to wiretapping. The cases also involve many different groups of people, from undocumented immigrants to American students.

In all of these cases, people want to protect their civil liberties. However, civil liberties are not black and white. The government considers national security and morality as well, and it weighs these concerns against personal freedoms. Every day, advocacy groups work to balance these issues with people's civil liberties.

The idea of justice is often shown as a blindfolded woman holding a set of scales to represent the impartial balance the courts must achieve in a fair decision.

CHAPTER 1

The United States and Civil Liberties

Americans have always been vocal about the protection of freedom. Since the country was founded, its citizens have fought to protect their own liberties. The American love of freedom is so well-known that people in other countries sometimes mention it to poke fun at Americans. Many Americans feel proud to live in a country with laws that protect their rights; however, just because those laws exist does not always mean they will be followed correctly.

In the 1700s, John Peter Zenger published the *New York Weekly Journal*. In his paper, Zenger criticized William Cosby, the governor of New York. Cosby had Zenger arrested for printing seditious and libelous material. Most people believed Zenger would be found guilty. However, attorney Andrew Hamilton defended Zenger and surprised everyone by winning the case in 1735. The jury supported freedom of the press by agreeing that Zenger had the right to print opinions that criticize government figures such as Cosby.

The right to a fair trial was upheld in the Boston Massacre trial. In 1770, British troops were stationed in Boston to keep the colonists from uprising. There was friction between the troops and the colonists. On March 5, a mob of colonists gathered around a group of British soldiers. The soldiers shot into the crowd because they thought they had been ordered to fire. They were put on trial for killing several colonists.

John Adams was an American who disliked many of Britain's actions in the colonies. However, he also was an attorney who believed in everyone's right to a fair trial. He agreed to represent the British soldiers in court. "Adams accepted, firm in the belief

… that no man in a free country should be denied the right to counsel and a fair trial,"[1] wrote historian David McCullough. Adams argued that if the soldiers were endangered by the mob, they had the legal right to fight back. The jury agreed with Adams and acquitted six of the soldiers. With this decision, the colonists upheld the belief that all people—even people they disliked—deserved a fair trial.

The Boston Massacre, shown here, was an important moment in U.S. history. The trial that followed set an expectation that favoritism would not be tolerated.

The U.S. Revolution for Civil Liberties

Some colonists felt that their natural rights were being abused by the British. The British taxed the colonists unfairly, seized their property, and harassed colonists who protested against Britain's policies. This is what started the American Revolution: Americans fought against the British for their freedom.

The Founding Fathers wrote the Declaration of Independence in 1776. They explained why America broke from Great Britain. According to the Declaration of Independence, people have natural rights that should not be abused by the government:

We hold these truths to be self-evident, that all men are created equal, that they are endowed by their Creator with certain unalienable Rights, that among these are Life, Liberty and the pursuit of Happiness. That to secure these rights, Governments are instituted among Men, deriving their just powers from the consent of the governed.

Americans won the war in 1783. After the war, the U.S. Constitution and the Bill of Rights were written and approved. These documents set up how the United States governs and how it protects citizens' liberties to this day.

Governing Documents

The U.S. Constitution was ratified in 1787. It is the framework of the U.S. government. It sets up the three branches of government and explains how they work together. The Constitution creates a strong national government.

Some Founding Fathers, such as James Madison, worried that a strong national government could violate citizens' freedoms, just as the British government had. "The essence of Government is power; and power, lodged as it must be in human hands, will ever be liable to abuse,"[2] Madison wrote. He wanted to add a bill of rights to the Constitution to protect people's freedoms from government abuse.

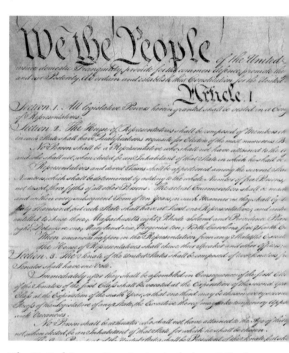

The United States Constitution includes a Bill of Rights that protects civil liberties for all citizens.

After the Constitution passed, Madison worked hard to get a bill of rights approved. He wrote his own set of amendments to the Constitution. The House of Representatives and Senate debated and altered these amendments, bringing the total to 12. These amendments were then sent to the states for approval. By 1791, all states had adopted 10 amendments to the Constitution, rejecting 2 of the ones Congress had proposed. These amendments are known as the Bill of Rights.

Rights of the People

In the United States, the Bill of Rights protects people's natural freedoms. It lists specific freedoms that the government cannot take away from people. These include the freedom of speech, the freedom of religion, the right to keep and bear arms, the freedom of assembly, and the freedom to petition.

FATHER OF LIBERTY

"The happy Union of these States is a wonder; their Constitution a miracle; their example the hope of Liberty throughout the world."
—James Madison, Founding Father and fourth president of the United States of America

Quoted in Samuel Sullivan Cox, *Eight Years in Congress, from 1857-1865: Memoir and Speeches.* D. Appleton and Company, New York, 1865, p. 314.

The Bill of Rights also restricts what the government can do to people. It protects people's privacy by restricting the government from unreasonable searches and seizures of people and their property. It prohibits the government from establishing a national religion. It does not allow the government to deprive any person of life, liberty, or property without due process of law. The Bill of Rights also protects those accused of crimes by guaranteeing people a speedy public trial by an unbiased jury.

Civil Liberties for All

Initially, the Bill of Rights applied only to the federal government. That meant that state and local governments could still make laws that violated the Bill of Rights and citizens' civil liberties. In 1833, the Supreme Court specifically ruled in the case of *Barron v. Baltimore* that the Bill of Rights applied only to the federal, and not any state, government.

This changed when the 14th Amendment was added to the Constitution following the American Civil War. It was one of three amendments added to secure the rights of former slaves. The 14th Amendment defines citizenship and guarantees that former U.S. slaves are citizens. It also guarantees due process and equal protection of each state's laws. The Supreme Court has interpreted this amendment to mean that state governments must follow the Bill of Rights.

The Bill of Rights applies to all citizens of the United States. It also applies to noncitizens who reside in the United States. The U.S. Constitution and Bill of Rights, state constitutions, and all laws apply to anyone within the country unless stated otherwise in the law itself. According to *Slate* magazine, "the Bill of Rights applies to everyone, even *illegal* immigrants. So an immigrant, legal or illegal, prosecuted under the criminal code has the right to due process, a speedy and public trial, and other rights protected by the Fifth and Sixth Amendments."[3]

Unprotected Citizens

Although the Bill of Rights applies to all people in the United States, the government has denied many groups of people their civil liberties. Until 1865, African Americans were kept as slaves in America. According to the ACLU,

> *Slavery was this country's original sin. For the first 78 years after it was ratified, the Constitution protected slavery and legalized racial subordination. Instead of constitutional rights, slaves were governed by "slave codes" that controlled every aspect of their lives. They had no access to the rule of law: they could not go to court, make contracts, or own any property. They could be whipped, branded, imprisoned without trial, and hanged.*[4]

The Civil War resulted in the abolishment of slavery. Amendments were added to the Constitution to protect the liberties of former slaves. The 13th Amendment officially put an end to slavery. The 14th Amendment guaranteed African Americans the right to due process and granted them citizenship. The 15th Amendment prevented the government from denying a person's right to vote because of his or her race.

Despite these changes, civil rights abuses continued. "Separate but equal" was a phrase used to describe segregation in the South. Blacks and whites had separate schools, restaurants, and other facilities. The Supreme Court heard *Plessy v. Ferguson* in 1896. This case concerned the segregation of blacks and whites on railroad cars. The Supreme Court upheld that separate but equal public facilities did not violate the Constitution. The Supreme Court, however, did not acknowledge that the separate facilities were not really equal; black facilities were substandard.

The 20th century brought some progress. The Supreme Court reversed its separate but equal ruling in 1954. In *Brown v. Board of Education*, the Court ruled that it was unconstitutional to create separate schools because of race. Following that case, the Supreme Court upheld federal laws that barred discrimination in other areas, such as public transportation. The Court also ruled that a state law against interracial marriage was invalid. From this point on, the government protected more of the civil liberties of African Americans. However, even today, the fight for the protection of African Americans' natural rights continues.

Although the Emancipation Proclamation of 1863 officially outlawed slavery in much of the United States, black people continue to fight for equality to this day.

Women and Equal Rights

Unlike African Americans, women in the United States are not a minority. They make up more than half of the country's population as of 2017. As a group, however, their rights have still been violated for centuries.

The right to own property is considered a civil liberty. Property rights include the legal rights to acquire, own, sell, and transfer property; collect and keep rents; keep one's wages; make contracts; and bring lawsuits. For years, women's property rights were denied. The husbands and fathers of women in the United States and most of the rest of the world controlled all property. This meant, for example, that if a man died and was survived by only daughters or a wife, they could not inherit the man's property. Everything he owned would go to his next male relative or heir, whether it was a nephew or distant cousin. The women of the family then had to rely on this person to provide for them. Without property, women could not control their own lives. They were dependent on men to survive.

In the United States, the 14th Amendment helped women fight for their rights. This amendment says that all persons, not just men, born in the United States are citizens. Being citizens gave women some power. With this power, they fought to protect their civil liberties. During the 19th century, many states passed laws to protect women's property rights. By 1900, every state gave married women substantial control over their property.

American women continued to fight for protection of their civil liberties, especially the right to vote. Susan B. Anthony was one of the earliest leaders of the women's movement. "It was we, the people; not we, the white male citizens; nor yet we, the male citizens; but we, the whole people, who formed the Union," said Anthony, referring to the words of the Constitution. "And we formed it, not to give the blessings of liberty, but to secure them; not to the half of ourselves and the half of our posterity, but to the whole people—women as well as men."[5]

The Women's Movement for Civil Liberties

During the 1800s, many women joined the fight against slavery. Some of these women became leaders in the movement, including Lucretia Mott and Elizabeth Cady Stanton. In 1840, Mott and Stanton traveled to London, England, to attend the World Anti-Slavery Convention. When they got there, Mott and Stanton were only allowed to listen to the conference from behind a curtain. They could not actively participate because they were women. This discrimination inspired them to organize the first women's rights convention, which met in 1848 in Seneca Falls, New York. More than 200 women and about 40 men attended. At the convention, Stanton and Mott presented the Declaration of Sentiments and Resolutions, a document that was based on the Declaration of Independence. The Declaration of Sentiments and Resolutions stated that men and women were created equal. Like men, women had natural rights.

The right to vote is a civil liberty, but women in most countries—including the United States—have had to fight long and hard to gain this right.

Women's Rights After 1920

The Woman's Suffrage Association was formed in 1890. This group focused almost exclusively on attaining the right to vote because without it, women could not affect the government's actions on issues that affected them. In 1920, the suffragettes won their battle, and the 19th Amendment was added to the Constitution.

Earning their own money also advanced women's rights. The Great Depression, which began with the October 1929 stock market crash, resulted in more women seeking paid work. By World War II, which the United States entered in 1941, up to 38 percent of American women were part of the workforce. The number of women in the workforce grew during the war as women took over the jobs of men who were sent to the front. As women's economic wealth grew, they became more confident. They banded together to fight for their natural rights.

Another victory for civil liberties came in 1964, when the government passed the Civil Rights Act. This act protected the rights of both women and African Americans. For example, it forbids sexual or racial discrimination in the workplace. Unfortunately, progress has not always continued so smoothly. For instance, the Equal Rights Amendment (ERA) was first proposed to Congress in 1923. It would be an amendment to the U.S. Constitution protecting equal rights for women, such as the right to be paid the same amount of money as a man who was doing the same job. The proposed amendment stated, "Equality of rights under the law shall not be denied or abridged by the United States or by any State on account of sex."[6] The amendment was denied for many years. It finally passed both houses of Congress in 1972, but a Constitutional amendment must also be ratified by the states. By 1979, activists against the ERA had convinced many states not to vote for the amendment. These activists, led by Phyllis Schlafly of the Eagle Forum/STOP (Stop Taking Our Privileges) ERA, claimed the ERA would take away the financial support of their husbands, allow women to serve in combat roles, and promote gay marriage. Some states agreed that these things were negative consequences of the bill, and the amendment was not passed. The amendment has been reintroduced by Congress every year since 1982.

Working to Protect Civil Liberties

In some cases, people have worked to protect their own civil rights. There are also organizations in the United States that work to protect civil liberties on behalf of all Americans. Roger Baldwin started the ACLU in 1920. The ACLU was, and still is, one of the nation's most prominent civil liberties groups.

One of the organization's first cases was about freedom of speech and freedom of religion. ACLU attorney Clarence Darrow defended John Scopes in *Tennessee v. John Scopes* in 1932. Scopes was a teacher who taught the theory of evolution in his class. This violated a state law that did not allow public schoolteachers to teach evolution theory. The law was in place because the evolution theory contradicted the biblical account of the world's

Roger Baldwin, shown here, started the ACLU to protect the rights of all people living in the United States.

creation. The ACLU claimed that the law violated religious freedom because the government, which runs the public schools, was supporting a religious belief. The law did not keep church and state issues separate. The ACLU said the Tennessee law also violated the freedom of speech by not allowing teachers to freely speak.

At the time, evolution was a controversial issue. Creationism was taught in many schools despite its religious basis, and it was supported by many people. Public rallies against the ACLU and its defense filled the streets in front of the courthouse. The judge, John Raulston, was a deeply religious man. He started the trial with a prayer and quoted scripture at different times throughout the proceedings. He also did not allow certain scientific testimony in support of evolution. The ACLU did not win the case, and Scopes was convicted. The trial, however, was famous, so it brought attention to the ACLU and to freedom of speech issues.

HUMAN RIGHTS IN ALL NATIONS

"All human beings are born free and equal in dignity and rights. They are endowed with reason and conscience and should act towards one another in a spirit of brotherhood."
—Article 1 of the United Nations' Universal Declaration of Human Rights

United Nations, "Universal Declaration of Human Rights." www.un.org/Overview/rights.html.

The ACLU went on to more prominent cases. In 1932, it organized the National Committee on Freedom from Censorship. This committee defended the freedom of expression as it fought censorship in the arts, press, movies, radio, and more. In 1933, it won a major ruling about censorship. The novel *Ulysses*, written by Irish author James Joyce, had been banned in the United States because it contained sexual content. People could not even bring the book into the country. The ACLU took this case to court and won: The court ruled that the book could no longer be taken away at U.S. borders.

The United Nations

Like the ACLU, the United Nations (UN) works to protect people's natural rights. It does so on a global level. In 1948, the UN issued the Universal Declaration of Human Rights, which states, "Everyone is entitled to all the rights and freedoms set forth in this Declaration, without distinction of any kind, such as race, color, sex, language, religion, political or other opinion, national or social origin, property, birth or other status."[1]

The declaration outlines 30 rights the United Nations believes all people have, such as free speech. It also includes the right to a life of security. People should not have to endure torture and violence. They should be able to live where they want to and not be restricted, meaning that governments should not regulate where a person can live. They should have the freedom to move to a different city or even a different country if they choose.

The UN's goal is to get all countries to protect these rights. In 1948, 48 countries, including the United States, voted in favor of this resolution. By 2008, 192 countries belonged to the United Nations. The organization's hope is that more governments around the world will continue to recognize and protect people's inherent rights.

1. United Nations, "The Universal Declaration of Human Rights," December 10, 1948. www.un.org/en/universal-declaration-human-rights/

The ACLU won a religious freedom case in 1943. At the time, public schools required all students to salute the U.S. flag. Jehovah's Witnesses did not want their children to salute the flag because they view it as worshipping an object. The ACLU argued that the requirement to salute the flag violated religious freedom. In the case, *West Virginia State Board of Education v. Barnette*, the Supreme Court ruled that Jehovah's Witnesses could refuse to salute the flag. Since then, the ACLU has continued to defend civil liberties. Today it continues to be one of the most prominent civil liberties organizations.

CHAPTER 2

Freedom of Speech

Freedom of speech is one of America's most treasured liberties, but it is sometimes misunderstood. The Bill of Rights protects Americans from being punished by the government for speaking their minds as long as they are not encouraging criminal activity, threatening others, or lying about people to get them in trouble. However, the First Amendment does not mean people are free from any and all consequences. Saying things that are racist, sexist, or otherwise objectionable may cause someone to lose their job or be kicked out of a club they belong to. This is not a violation of free speech because private organizations are allowed to decide who they want to be associated with. Similarly, if a publication prints something many people dislike, it is not a violation of free speech for people to cancel their subscriptions or for advertisers to stop supporting the publication.

However, freedom of speech does protect people who seek political change by criticizing the government and its policies. This is important because if the First Amendment did not exist in the United States, the government would be able to arrest anyone who said something it objected to. People would be afraid to speak up, and social problems would never be solved. "The beauty of free speech is that it serves as the ultimate protection of minority viewpoints, ensuring that no matter the political tide, all people will be allowed to speak their minds,"[7] wrote Robert Shibley, vice president of the Foundation for Individual Rights in Education.

As an example, during the 2016 presidential campaign, people wrote and spoke their opinions about presidential candidates Hillary Clinton and Donald Trump. Some opinions were very critical of the candidates. People also openly expressed their opinions about many issues. Americans could read and listen to all of these opinions and then make their personal choices with their votes.

Freedom of speech protects people from being punished by the government for most of the things they say.

Restricted Speech

Not all countries protect free speech or free press. In some countries, people are restricted in what they can say or write. Typically, governments restrict free speech because government leaders do not want to be questioned. They want to rule their way, with no criticism or opposition.

Iran is a country that restricts free expression. The Iranian government restricts reporters and visitors from other nations. Visitors can be jailed for questioning or criticizing the government. One recent example is Jason Rezaian, who held dual citizenship in Iran and the United States. He was serving as a reporter for the *Washington Post* when he was arrested. Rezaian spent 545 days in jail on unspecified charges. Iran denied him the right to meet with his lawyer or understand the charges against him. With the help of the United States, Rezaian was released in January 2016.

PROTECTING AMERICAN SPEECH ABROAD

"For much of the 18 months I was in prison, my Iranian interrogators told me the *Washington Post* did not exist, that no one knew of my plight and that the United States government would not lift a finger for my release ...Today, I'm here in this room with the very people who helped prove the Iranians wrong in so many ways ... No other country would do so much for an ordinary citizen."

–Jason Rezaian, journalist

Quoted in Tom Kludt, "Jason Rezaian: Iranian Captors Told Me Help Wasn't on the Way," CNN, January 28, 2016. money.cnn.com/2016/01/28/media/jason-rezaian-washington-post/.

Some countries, such as China, claim to protect free speech. China's constitution states, "Citizens of the People's Republic of China enjoy freedom of speech, of the press, of assembly, of association, of procession and of demonstration."[8] In practice, though, free speech is not protected in China. The government does not allow citizens to openly criticize its policies. Discussion of controversial subjects is restricted on the Internet in China, as well.

Restrictions to Civil Liberties in the U.S.

Even in countries that protect free expression, there are limits. The freedom of speech is a fundamental right, but it is not absolute. Most democratic countries allow as much free speech as possible. However, there are some restrictions to keep order. For example, people cannot use speech to cause violence or chaos.

In the United States, people are restricted from saying "fighting words"—words that are meant to inflict injury and incite violence—to another person. This restriction came from a New Hampshire court case that made it to the Supreme Court. A New Hampshire court convicted a man for making offensive comments to a city official. He violated a state law that did not allow people to use insulting language toward people in public places. In 1942, the Supreme Court heard his case, *Chaplinsky v. New Hampshire*. The Court upheld the state's decision to convict Chaplinsky. According to the majority opinion, "There are certain well-defined and narrowly limited classes of speech, the prevention and punishment of which have never been thought to raise any constitutional problem. These include … 'fighting' words—those which by their very utterance inflict injury or tend to incite an immediate breach of the peace."[9]

Freedom of Speech

Americans express their opinions in many ways. In Arizona, the members of the Arizona Life Coalition, an antiabortion group, decided to show their opinions on license plates. They tried to order specialty license plates with the slogan "Choose Life" on them. The state refused to fill the organization's order. In the past, the state license plate commission had approved plates for other nonprofit organizations, such as police and firefighter associations and the Wildlife Conservation Council. When the case went to court, a federal judge ruled in the state's favor. The judge said that because the message was on state-issued license plates, the government could control the plates' content. In 2008, the U.S. Court of Appeals for the Ninth Circuit, based in San Francisco, California, heard the case's appeal. It overturned the federal court and ruled in favor of the Arizona Life Coalition. The court said that the slogan is private speech by the organization, not the government. The court went on to say that when the state denied the plates, it restricted free speech. Today, the plates with the "Choose Life" slogan are available in Arizona.

It is not always easy to determine what can be considered fighting words. For example, some people believe that all hate speech should be considered fighting words. Hate speech refers to words meant to cause prejudice against a person or group of people based on their race, religion, nationality, or other factors. Other people do not consider hate speech fighting words. According to these people, hate speech may be offensive, but if it does not cause violence or illegal actions, then it is still protected by the Constitution.

Many college campuses have codes that restrict hate speech. The codes typically prohibit speech that offends any group. For example, in the Texas A&M University system, all campuses follow a code that requires students to respect other students' personal feelings and their right to freedom from indignity. The code does not specify what actions are considered violations of these rights, leaving it up to each university to decide on a case-by-case basis. If a student believes the code has been violated, he or she contacts the dean of student life for a review of the situation. The severity of the incident determines the action. If the offensive conduct is protected speech but contradicts the Texas A&M University code, the university states that the students' constitutional rights will continue to be protected. However, university staff have the right to discuss these behaviors with the students.

Civil liberties organizations such as the ACLU fight against speech codes. They believe all speech, even hate speech, is protected by the Bill of Rights and that if one group is silenced, it is possible for the government to justify silencing other groups. The ACLU argues that if hate speech is allowed, people can debate it and come to their own opinion about it:

> Where racist, sexist and homophobic speech is concerned, the ACLU believes that more speech—not less—is the best revenge. This is particularly true at universities, whose mission is to facilitate learning through open debate and study, and to enlighten. Speech codes are not the way to go on campuses, where all views are entitled to be heard, explored, supported or refuted. Besides, when hate is out in the open, people can see the problem. Then they can organize effectively to counter bad attitudes, possibly change them, and forge solidarity against the forces of intolerance.[10]

Open discussion of ideas can help everyone understand why some speech, though protected, can be considered hateful and should be avoided out of respect for others. Just because something is legal does not always mean it is the right thing to do.

Standing Up for Rights

A public protest is when people gather together and promote their beliefs. Protesters hope to persuade other people to support their opinions. Often people protest against decisions the government has made in an effort to get the decision reversed. In the United States, people can voice their opinions in a public forum and openly criticize the government because the First Amendment also protects the freedom to assemble and the freedom of speech.

American protests date back to the Boston Tea Party prior to the American Revolution, when colonists boarded a ship and dumped the cargo of tea into the water to protest the British tax on tea. Protests have continued throughout American history.

Protests were very common during the 1960s. Some people protested against the unjust treatment of black people. Others protested for women's rights. Many protested against the United States fighting in the Vietnam War. "Americans were increasingly less content with the actions of the government and the authority. Migrant workers held strikes, students conducted sit-ins, African-Americans performed non-violent resistance and people marched," wrote Chris Gauthier of the Massachusetts College of Liberal Arts. "These forms of protest brought people with common causes together, and gave a voice to many who were voiceless."[11]

Protests often result in heated feelings on both sides. Because of these feelings, sometimes protests become violent. Although protests are protected by the Constitution, protestors can be arrested if they break other laws. For example, a protest on January 20, 2017, turned violent. A large, unorganized group of peaceful protestors marched in Washington, D.C., to protest a variety of issues, such as racism and immigrants' rights. Nearby, a small group of people who had been involved in an earlier march were cornered by police because the small group of protestors had broken windows and caused other property destruction. The peaceful marchers circled the police and demanded that they release the small group of people who were being detained. Writer Robin Seemangal described what happened next:

The ordeal lasted about an hour, and the demonstration attracted those who had no intention of keeping the peace ... They taunted the police and called for violence against them.

The peaceful protestors began to try and shout them down, calling for peace. But more and more of these self-proclaimed anarchists began to show up and be disruptive, and even inciteful. Things seemed to be looking up when another march made its way to the corner to magnify the voice of the crowd calling for the release of those detained. But as soon as they got there, the area became unsafe for everyone. I'm unclear as to what exactly ignited the chaos, but one moment I was shooting a video on my phone, and the next, I was being burned by pepper spray.[12]

This incident shows that although protests are protected under the Constitution, they can sometimes become dangerous. Even peaceful protestors may be at risk for violence when police feel threatened. It is crucial for protestors to understand the importance of following laws when they demonstrate to reduce the risk of violence for all involved.

Protected Mediums for Expression

Groups such as the American Academy of Pediatrics and the American Medical Association are concerned that violent entertainment, such as books, music, and video games, can lead to violence. In particular, they are concerned that young people may commit violent acts after exposure to violent entertainment. There have been a number of studies on children's exposure to violent games. There is no conclusive link between violent media and violent behavior, but some studies point to an increase in aggression by children exposed to violence. As a result, many people believe that the government should limit the violent content in certain forms of entertainment.

Limiting the free expression of video games, television, and other entertainment has become more of an issue as school violence has increased. In the past three decades, there have been a number of incidents in which students have shot classmates and teachers. The National Institute of Justice reported that "theft, violent crime and student homicides in American schools (with children in grades K-12) have declined over the past decade,"[13] but violent incidents still occur, which worries many people. Many still believe that fights, gang violence, and school shootings have increased across the country, despite the decline in actual numbers. In search of an explanation for why these events keep happening, some people have pointed to violence in books, movies, television, and video games.

Video games are one of the more controversial forms of entertainment. This is because some simulate graphic violence. Many video games are in a category called "first-person shooter." These games, such as the Call of Duty games, allow the player to commit violence from the point of view of a gunman. The game is visually realistic and violently explicit. After the 2012 school shooting at Sandy Hook Elementary, police found that the shooter, Adam Lanza, was an avid player of the Call of Duty games. They also found that he played a nonviolent video game, *Dance Dance Revolution*, more than any other game, but played even this game aggressively.

Because of concerns about video games, such as the Call of Duty and Grand Theft Auto games, the U.S. video game industry has developed its own ratings system. A game rated "Teen" is

Some people believe that first-person shooter games such as the Call of Duty series encourage real-life violence among young adults.

for ages 13 and up. "Mature" ratings are for games considered suitable only for ages 17 and older and may include more intense violence, profanity, and mature sexual themes. "Adults Only" games are intended for people older than 18 and may include graphic depictions of sex and violence. It is not illegal for minors, or people under the age of 18, to buy these games, but many retailers refuse to sell adult-rated games to minors who do not have parental permission.

Some states did pass laws that banned the sale of violent video games to minors. The courts, however, have overruled these laws. For example, in 2011, California tried to ban the sale of violent video games to minors, but the Supreme Court ruled that this was unconstitutional. Although debate about violent entertainment continues, to date, the courts have supported that video games showing violence are protected by the Constitution.

Morality and Free Expression

Free expression is sometimes limited if it is considered indecent by some. The difficulty with this concept is determining what is decent and what is not. Who sets the standard? Countries that protect free expression try to balance decency and freedom.

The U.S. courts have ruled that the First Amendment protects indecent material. It cannot be banned entirely; however, it may be restricted to protect children. The Federal Communications Commission (FCC), a government organization that regulates television, radio, and the Internet, restricts what can be aired on broadcast television and radio stations and at what time. For example, indecent material cannot be aired during the day when young children may be watching.

Obscenity and child pornography, however, are not protected by the First Amendment. The government can restrict its availability to everyone. The Supreme Court ruled that the First Amendment does not protect obscenity during the *Miller v. California* case in 1973, when Marvin Miller, the owner of a pornographic mail-order company, was convicted for mailing out brochures with pornography on them to advertise his business. The Court also developed "the Miller test" to decide if something is obscene. There are three conditions that must be met.

The first is that most average people would consider the work offensive. The second is that the work depicts or describes sexual conduct or bodily functions in an offensive way. The third is that the work, as a whole, lacks serious literary, artistic, political, or scientific value.

THE DEFINITIVE EDITION

THE DIARY OF A YOUNG GIRL

ANNE FRANK

Anne Frank's The Diary of a Young Girl *is one book that has been banned in the United States. However, it was not banned by the government, only by some private institutions.*

Restricting Information

Book banning is a form of censorship that has been debated for nearly as long as books have existed. It occurs in countries with a lot of government restriction, as well as countries with a lot of freedom. "Banning books isn't something that was done centuries or decades ago. It happens nearly every week somewhere in the United States," stated the publisher Adler and Robin Books. "Often people take notice of banned books, protest, and the proscription is lifted. Sometimes nobody notices and the banned book stays lost to a school or county."[14] Classics such as *To Kill a Mockingbird*, Anne Frank's *Diary of a Young Girl*, and *Huckleberry Finn* have been banned from libraries and schools because people have disagreed with their content.

The Supreme Court has ruled that banning books in public schools violates the

First Amendment. This is because the government funds public schools, and an agency supported by the government cannot interfere with free expression. "Local school boards may not remove books from school library shelves simply because they dislike the ideas contained in those books,"[15] wrote the Supreme Court in 1982. This was decided during the *Board of Education, Island Trees School District v. Pico* case. The Supreme Court ruled that school boards are restricted in what books they can remove.

Another book banning case went to court in 2003. An Arkansas school board voted to remove all of the books in J.K. Rowling's Harry Potter series from the district's public school libraries because they "include witchcraft and the occult and also encourage disobedience and disrespect for authority."[16] Students could only check out these books with written parental permission. Students and parents filed a case because they wanted the books returned to the shelves. The Arkansas judge ordered the books returned to the library shelves, ruling that books could not be banned just because some people disagreed with their content.

FREEDOM IS LIKE AIR

"One of the strange things about free speech is if you live in a free society in which, broadly speaking, you have free speech, you don't think about it that often. Just like if there's enough air, you don't think about the air."
-Salman Rushdie, author and target of censorship

Quoted in Ashutosh Varsney, "The Political Rushdie," *Journal of the International Institute*, vol. 10, issue 3, Spring/Summer 2003. quod.lib.umich.edu/j/jii/4750978.0010.306/--political-rushdie?rgn=main;view=fulltext.

Cyber Restrictions

The Internet has brought about new free speech issues. People can post and view anything they want on the Internet. Some people believe that what can be placed online should be limited. They are concerned that children can go on the Internet and see indecent and even obscene material.

There are laws in place to help prevent people under the age of 18 from seeing pornographic images online.

Because of this concern, the U.S. Congress passed the Communications Decency Act in 1996. This law was meant to protect minors from harmful material on the Internet. Specifically, the law made it a crime to post indecent or clearly offensive material anywhere a minor could see it.

Free speech advocates brought the case to court in *Reno v. American Civil Liberties Union*. They were against the part of the act that related to indecent, not obscene, material. They argued that indecent expression is protected under the First Amendment; therefore, it should have no restrictions on the Internet. The Supreme Court heard the case in 1997. It ruled that restricting the posting of indecent material on the Internet was unconstitutional because it forced the removal of material that adults had a right to see.

Three years later, Congress passed another law that restricts Internet access. The courts upheld this law. The Children's Internet Protection Act (CIPA) states that government-funded schools and libraries must filter obscene pictures and pornography shown on the Internet. In 2003, the Supreme Court heard a case about CIPA. The Court stated that filters do not violate the Constitution, especially since libraries could turn off the filters upon request.

Another threat to free speech on the Internet is the concept of net neutrality—rules put in place to prevent Internet service providers (ISPs) from charging more for certain content. In February 2015, the FCC ruled in favor of net neutrality; as *USA Today* explained, "An ISP will be prohibited from slowing the delivery of a TV show simply because it's streamed by a video company that competes with a subsidiary [company owned by] the ISP."[17] Several ISPs protested the ruling, claiming that net neutrality unconstitutionally limits what they can do as a company. However, individual citizens cheered the ruling because they were worried ISPs would begin limiting content they did not agree with, taking the power of Internet surfing out of the hands of individuals.

A New Platform for Free Speech

Since the creation of easy-to-use blogs in 1999, people have been posting their thoughts online about every topic in the world. Some believe that a blogger should be able to post anything that he or she wants to and be protected by the First Amendment. "Freedom of speech is the foundation of a functioning democracy, and Internet bullies shouldn't use the law to stifle legitimate free expression,"[1] wrote the Electronic Frontier Foundation. However, bloggers must follow the same laws as the media. These include respecting privacy and copyrights and not committing libel, which means spreading lies about someone to ruin their reputation. One problem is that, unlike media professionals, most bloggers do not know or understand all the laws. Another problem is that it is easy for bloggers to get away with not following the law if they so choose. Because so many people publish on the Internet and at such great speed, it is hard to stop illegal actions.

1. "EFF: Legal Guide for Bloggers," Electronic Frontier Foundation, April 20, 2006. w2.eff.org/bloggers/lg.

A Free Press and Media

Free press is another civil liberty that falls under the freedom of expression. In the United States and most democracies, freedom of the press is guaranteed. This means the government cannot interfere with what newspapers, magazines, or television news programs report.

Not all countries support freedom of the press. Many countries crack down on reporters who write or say anything critical of government officials or policies. In fact, more than a third of all people in the world live in countries without free press. In these countries, it is often dangerous to report unflattering news.

According to the International News Safety Institute, 115 journalists were killed around the world in 2016. Hundreds more were threatened, imprisoned, or tortured. Some of this violence was because reporters were reporting news not approved by the government.

Although the United States guarantees free press, there are some restrictions. The media cannot maliciously libel or slander a person. When it comes to respecting privacy, courts have generally ruled that journalists have the right to report anything that is arguably of interest to their readers. However, what is of interest is up for debate. In some court cases about privacy, the rulings have favored the press; in others, they have favored the person who feels his or her privacy has been invaded.

Overall, the United States maintains freedom of the press. According to Vince Crawley, a staff writer in the Bureau of International Information Programs of the U.S. Department of State, "A free and independent press provides people with the information they need to play an active role in the government and life of their country and people must have the freedom to speak their mind and to publish criticism of their government."[18] Americans believe that freedom of the press, along with the right to assemble and freedom of speech, keeps the United States in the hands of the people.

Freedom of the press protects newspapers and magazines from being targeted by the government as long as the facts they print are true.

CHAPTER 3

Freedom of Religion

In 2014, the Pew Forum on Religion and Public Life found that 89 percent of Americans believe in God, which was down from 92 percent in 2007. People in the United States follow a variety of spiritual paths—Christianity, Judaism, Hinduism, Islam, Buddhism, paganism, and more. The government protects the right of its citizens to freely practice any of these faiths or no faith at all. Freedom of religion also means the government is not allowed to make laws based on any religion. This protects people who do not follow a particular religion from being forced to abide by laws they may not believe in.

Religious Landscape

United States, 2014

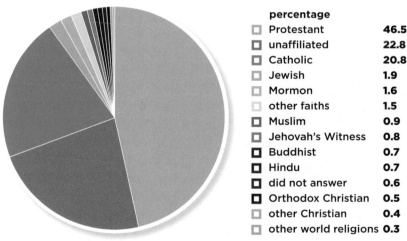

	percentage
Protestant	**46.5**
unaffiliated	**22.8**
Catholic	**20.8**
Jewish	**1.9**
Mormon	**1.6**
other faiths	**1.5**
Muslim	**0.9**
Jehovah's Witness	**0.8**
Buddhist	**0.7**
Hindu	**0.7**
did not answer	**0.6**
Orthodox Christian	**0.5**
other Christian	**0.4**
other world religions	**0.3**

People of different faiths are free to worship in the United States, as this information from the Pew Research Center shows. The "other faiths" category includes Unitarians, New Age, and Native American religions; the "other world religions" category includes Sikhs, Taoists, and Jains.

Other countries also protect religious freedom. Most of these nations are democracies. Many countries, such as the United States, attempt to keep the government and religion completely separate. Other countries protect religious freedom but still allow religion to play a role in the government. For example, Denmark guarantees religious freedom, but it also recognizes a state religion. This means that its state church, the Church of Denmark, gets certain benefits, such as tax breaks, that other churches do not. Also, Denmark's schools provide religious instruction in the official state religion. However, students may be excused from religion classes with parental permission. Denmark's government permits religious practices other than the state religion. It does not persecute believers of other faiths.

No Freedom for Religion

Not all countries protect religious freedom. In certain countries, citizens must follow the government-sanctioned religion. In these countries, religion is often tied to how the country is run. In Saudi Arabia, for example, the Qur'an—the Muslim holy book—is the constitution of the country. By law, all Saudi citizens must be Muslims and follow the laws of the Qur'an. The government punishes those who practice other religions.

China is another country with little religious freedom. Officially, China guarantees freedom of religion under its constitution, but religions must be approved and religious gatherings must be supervised by government officials. Some groups meet secretly, but they may be arrested if they are discovered. In recent years, the Chinese government has faced more accusations that it is limiting Christians' religious freedom. According to CBS, "One provincial government has systematically removed crosses from churches. [In February 2016], a Protestant pastor was sentenced to 14 years in prison, convicted of financial crimes and also for illegally gathering people to disturb social order."[19]

Civil liberties organizations believe that the Chinese government limits religious practices because it fears that religion threatens government security. "The ruling Communist Party perceives unregulated religious activity as a threat to its power,"

Some Chinese people protest the government's restriction of religion. This woman's sign calls for the release of Christian church officials who were targeted by the Chinese government.

reported the International Coalition for Religious Freedom. "They are alarmed by a growing association between many pro-democracy dissidents and underground churches. The government fears foreign influence through religious groups with international association."[20] China counters that it safeguards religious freedom, but religious organizations must follow the laws of the country, which include registering the organization through the government and following the government's procedures. This, the government claims, protects both religious freedom and national order.

DECLARING THE FREEDOMS

"[The Declaration of Independence] marked the beginning of the end of the religious state and the emergence of the secular state based on the consent of the governed, rather than the revealed word of God."
–Alan Dershowitz, professor of law at Harvard Law School

Alan Dershowitz, *Blasphemy*. New Jersey: John Wiley & Sons, 2007, p. 67.

The Constitution and Religious Freedom

Americans enjoy religious freedom because the Constitution protects this civil liberty. The First Amendment of the Bill of Rights prevents the government from interfering in a person's religious choices. The first clause of the amendment is the Establishment Clause, which states that "Congress shall make no law respecting an establishment of religion." This means that the government cannot set up a state religion. It also cannot give privileges to one religion over another. This is often referred to as the separation of church and state, or secularism.

Burkinis in France

Some countries try to limit religion in public. Many places have tried to ban religious dress, especially focusing on Muslim head scarves (hijabs) or full-body coverings (burkas). In 2016, some French beach towns restricted the right of women to wear a burkini, a type of modest swimwear that covers the body and hair. The ban was said to protect secularism. Many women in burkinis were fined and told to leave the beaches. One woman was made to take off her covering in front of the police. Knowledge of the ban spread through the Western world, leading to demonstrations from Muslims and women in France and around the world. People declared the ban to be an infringement of the rights of people to dress how they like as well as an infringement of religious freedom. The highest court in France agreed and quickly overturned the ban, stating that it violated civil liberties.

Shown here is a woman in a burkini, a type of bathing suit that is controversial in France.

The First Amendment continues with the Free Exercise Clause. This clause forbids Congress from "prohibiting the free exercise [of religion]." This part of the amendment means that the government cannot interfere with a person's religious practices as long as the practices are legal.

One difficulty with these clauses is that they can clash. On one side, the government must try to ensure that people can freely practice their religions. On the other side, the government has to be sure that it does not promote a certain religion when protecting this right. Keeping this balance is not always easy.

School Prayer

The two clauses of the First Amendment can be at odds when it comes to school prayer. Some public schools—schools that are funded by the government—devote a few minutes each day to silent prayer. Many people believe that school prayer is a right guaranteed by the Free Exercise Clause.

Others believe school prayer is a violation of the Establishment Clause. They think that if a public school devotes time to prayer, it is an example of the government imposing religion on students. The American courts have ruled on the matter. They have stated that mandated school prayer in public schools violates the First Amendment. However, courts have allowed a moment of silence in public schools, and students are allowed to pray silently to themselves; religion is permitted as long as no one is forced into doing something they do not want to do. In 2000, Virginia enacted a law that required a moment of silence. Students may choose to pray, meditate, or just sit quietly during this time. Some parents and students challenged this law, claiming it was unconstitutional because even a moment of silence implies prayer and promotes religion. The case went to a federal appeals court. The court found that the law did not violate the First Amendment because the law did not require prayer or promote it.

Religion in Public Schools

Another religious matter—whether to teach creationism, evolution, or both—has been an ongoing debate in schools. Creationism is the belief that God created the world exactly as stated in the Bible. Creationists get this belief from some Christian religious teachings. Evolution is a scientific theory that all life today is the result of many changes that have happened over millions of years. This is based on scientific evidence and research.

Some parents believe that evolution conflicts with their religious beliefs. They think that their children should not be taught about evolution. Other parents believe that creationism should not be taught in public schools. They think this is the government mandating religion.

For years, teachers taught creationism in schools without controversy. However, when scientists such as Charles Darwin made great strides in understanding the development of humans and the natural world, evolutionary science advanced. By the 1900s, more people wanted evolution taught in public schools. However, many religious people were offended by the theory of evolution. By 1925, some states had passed laws that made it illegal to teach evolution in schools. As the years passed, the laws against evolution were contested, and eventually the courts overturned them. They allowed for evolution to be taught to students because it is a scientific theory. Then, the Supreme Court ruled that public schools could not teach creationism as a scientific view of the world's beginnings. Because creationism is a religious view, it violates the Establishment Clause. However, creationism can be discussed in classes about religious theory. "Educators may not teach, as fact, the theory that humankind was created by a divine being. In science classes, educators must present only scientific explanations for life on earth and scientific critiques of evolution," wrote the Anti-Defamation League. "Furthermore, schools may not refuse to teach evolution in an effort to avoid offending religious individuals."[21]

Religion and State

Despite the separation of church and state, the American government refers to God in some of its documents. The Declaration of Independence discusses a so-called creator. American dollar bills include the words "In God We Trust." The Pledge of Allegiance, an oath of allegiance that Americans say in support of the United States, includes the words "under God." For this reason in particular, the pledge has brought about controversy. The original Pledge of Allegiance did not include reference to God, even though it was written by a Baptist minister in 1892. In 1954, the U.S. Congress agreed to insert the words "under God" because of people's fear of Communism during what was known as the Cold War with the Soviet Union. It was generally thought at that time that Communists did not believe in God.

Many public schools devote time in the morning to reciting the pledge. The controversy is that some parents believe that reciting the pledge violates the Establishment Clause. They feel that a public school should not make students recite a pledge with God in it. By doing so, they reason, the government is imposing religion on people. Others believe that the pledge is not religious and reciting "under God" is just a tradition.

NO SUPPORT FOR LEGAL PREFERENCE

"I am for freedom of religion, and against all maneuvers to bring about a legal ascendancy of one sect over another."
–Thomas Jefferson, Founding Father and third president of the United States

Quoted in Saul K. Padover, *Thomas Jefferson and the Foundations of American Freedom.* Princeton, NJ: D. van Nostrand Company, Inc., p. 119.

In 1943, the Supreme Court heard *West Virginia Board of Education v. Barnette.* Since the words "under God" had not yet been added at this point, the case was not about religious freedom; it was about whether students should be required to recite the pledge at all. The Court ruled that students should be able to opt out of the pledge. Although students have this right, some people still feel that saying it at school violates the Establishment Clause. Cases regarding the pledge continue to go to court. In 2014, a New Jersey family and the American Humanist Society filed to have "under God" removed from the pledge, stating that it "marginalizes atheist and humanist kids as something less than ideal patriots."[22] They lost the case in 2015, when a state judge ruled in favor of the school district and Samantha Jones, a teen who argued that removing the words from the pledge would take away her right to say the pledge in full.

Religion in the Classroom

Another religious issue in schools is how to preserve students' personal freedom to express their beliefs while not inflicting their views on their classmates. Basically, students can express their beliefs in their homework, artwork, and other assignments. They can talk about religious beliefs with their classmates. Students can pray at school as long as it does not interfere with school functions. They can wear clothing that expresses their religious viewpoints.

Students can also set up religious clubs. The Equal Access Act, passed in the United States in 1984, states that if a school receives federal aid and has at least one student-led non-curriculum club that meets outside of class time, it must allow other such clubs to be organized. These clubs may be religious.

In the United States, the religious freedom of teachers is also guaranteed in schools. They can pray and read the Bible or other religious works as long as they do so privately and on their own time. Additionally, they cannot impose their beliefs on others. They may discuss religion in class, but it must be pertinent to the subject.

Students are allowed to pray quietly in public schools if they wish. Forcing someone to pray and banning someone from praying are both violations of civil liberties.

Basically, public school teachers cannot teach students what to believe. However, teachers can teach about religion. According to "A Teacher's Guide to Religion in the Public Schools," "Religion must be taught objectively and neutrally. The purpose of public schools is to educate students about a variety of religious traditions, not to indoctrinate them into any tradition."[23] This means that teachers can discuss religions if they are related to the subject. For example, they can discuss the Bible in terms of history and culture. However, they must never promote one particular religion as the truth.

Public Versus Private Schools

Public schools receive money from the government, so they must follow the rules decided on by the courts. However, private schools are funded by the parents of the children who attend them, so those students' rights are not protected by the Constitution. Things that are not allowed in public schools, such as mandatory prayer, restrictions on free speech, and discrimination based on sexual orientation can be allowed in a private school. However, this does not mean private schools allow everything public schools do not; as in public schools, it is illegal for staff to hurt students, and schools are not allowed to deny students entry based on race. Additionally, each state has its own rules regarding private schools. For instance, New York State requires all students attending high school to take standardized tests called the Regents Examinations before they can graduate, whether the school is private or public. Most other states do not regulate private schools' testing policies.

Taxpayer Money for Religious Schools

Another heated issue regarding religion and education involves school vouchers. A school voucher is a certificate issued by the government that parents can use to send their children to a school of their choice, including private schools. One reason why school vouchers are controversial is because parents have used them to send their children to religious schools.

Some people believe that once the government gives parents the voucher, it is up to the parents to determine whether they want their children to receive a religious education. Others believe that government funding should not be used to support religious schools in any way. "Alongside reading and writing, many parochial schools include a generous dollop of religious indoctrination … This is perfectly fine—so long as it is underwritten with private funds," wrote Reverend Barry Lynn, a member of Americans United for Separation of Church and State. "When it occurs with tax funds taken from people of many different faiths, it is, no matter how one tries to mask it, forced support for religion."[24]

The Supreme Court has upheld the constitutionality of school vouchers. In 2002, the Court heard a case about school vouchers in Cleveland that centered on whether using public money for religious schools violates the First Amendment. The Court ruled that it did not because of the school choices. "In sum, the Ohio program is entirely neutral with respect to religion," Chief Justice William H. Rehnquist wrote in his majority opinion. "It provides benefits directly to a wide spectrum of individuals, defined only by financial need and residence in a particular school district."[25]

Religious Displays

Holiday displays are at the heart of another issue regarding the separation of church and state. "Each year as the winter holidays approach, Americans across the country debate the appropriateness of the government sponsoring, or even permitting, the display of Christmas nativity scenes, Hanukkah menorahs and other religious holiday symbols on public property,"[26] wrote the Pew Forum on Religion and Public Life. Some people believe that these displays are harmless celebrations of the holiday season. Other people argue that the displays mean that the government is sponsoring religion.

The Supreme Court first heard a case about public religious displays in 1980. The case was about a Kentucky law that required public schools to display the Ten Commandments. The court determined that the law was government sponsorship of religion, and it was ruled unconstitutional. In another religious display case four years later, there was a different outcome. In this case, the Court ruled that a Christmas nativity scene displayed in the municipal square of Pawtucket, Rhode Island, was acceptable. The Court reasoned that the scene recognized the history of Christmas, and it noted that Christmas has both secular and religious significance. The justices concluded that the display did not mean that the government endorsed Christianity.

Since then, courts throughout the United States have heard more cases about religious displays. The courts have ruled differently in different cases. Some justices believe in a strict separation of church and state, so they tend to rule that any government-sponsored religious displays violate the Establishment Clause. Other justices argue that, because of the role that religion has played in U.S. history, the government can display a variety of religious symbols for historical purposes.

The conflict between the court's justices reflects the conflict Americans feel about church-and-state issues. According to the Pew Research Center, 44 percent of American adults believe Christian symbols should be allowed on government property. Another 28 percent say Christian symbols should be allowed only if they are accompanied by symbols from other faiths; for instance, they believe if a government building is going to have a nativity scene outside, it should also have a menorah. Only 20 percent of Americans believe religious symbols should be completely banned from government property.

The First Amendment provides the guidance for how issues should be treated, but it can be interpreted in different ways. The U.S. government strives to follow the amendment's guidance, balancing both clauses.

Shown here is a nativity scene outside the U.S. Supreme Court Building, which is a government building. Some Americans believe this is acceptable; others do not.

CHAPTER 4

Civil Liberties and National Security

Civil liberties become even more controversial when they concern matters of national security. Some people support measures they believe will help the government keep citizens safe, even when those measures violate civil liberties. This is especially true in the case of terrorism; many Americans fear terrorists and believe the government should be able to investigate anyone for any reason if it helps catch terrorists before they can hatch a plot. These people generally feel that government surveillance is not a problem because innocent people have nothing to hide and therefore, nothing to fear from the government.

However, many others believe that there is no excuse for violating people's rights in the name of national security. They fear that if the government has unrestricted access to their information, they may be vulnerable to being arrested for crimes they did not even know they were committing. For instance, marijuana use is legal in several states but is still a federal crime. A person in Colorado—one of the states where marijuana is legal for both medical and recreational use—who e-mails a friend about what kind of marijuana they purchased may be at risk for arrest by the federal government. Generally, the federal government does not prosecute private citizens for marijuana use in states where it has been legalized, but it can if it chooses to. While marijuana use is not related to terrorism, the government may find this information while investigating people for possible terrorist activities.

Throughout history, the U.S. government has limited civil liberties in order to maintain national security. This has occurred most often during times of war or threat of war. Often, the restrictions were repealed when the threat was over. As early as 1798, the United States passed a law to restrict freedoms. During that year, the country was on the verge of war with France, and the Alien and Sedition Acts were signed into law. Proponents of the acts claimed they were needed to suppress French sympathizers and their attempts to weaken the U.S. government. Because of the acts, people were jailed if they published anything malicious about the U.S. government. When the threat of war was over, the acts were repealed.

The U.S. government continued to restrict freedoms during war times, however. In 1861, President Abraham Lincoln suspended habeas corpus, which is a legal action that protects people from being unlawfully detained or held in prison without charges being filed and without giving the accused some recourse to address the charges. The writ of habeas corpus has historically been used to protect an individual's freedom against government detention.

President Lincoln suspended this protection during the Civil War because people were rioting and rebelling against the war. This action allowed the military to detain people it thought threatened the country's security even if they could not be charged with a crime. Lincoln declared,

> Now, therefore, be it ordered, that during the existing insurrection, and as a necessary measure for suppressing the same, all rebels and insurgents, their aiders and abettors within the United States, and all persons discouraging volunteer enlistments, resisting militia drafts, or guilty of any disloyal practice affording aid and comfort to the rebels against the authority of the United States, shall be subject to martial law, and liable to trial and punishment by courts-martial or military commission.[27]

The courts reinstated habeas corpus after the Civil War.

Violations in the 20th Century

The U.S. government passed another sedition act in 1918, during World War I. Then, after the war, Communists took control of Russia, and some Americans supported the Communist Party in the United States. Americans became afraid of Communists who lived in the country. Many believed that Communists wanted to overthrow the American government. "The nation was gripped in fear," wrote Paul Burnett of the University of Missouri, Kansas City, School of Law. "Innocent people were jailed for expressing their views, civil liberties were ignored, and many Americans feared that a Bolshevik-style revolution was at hand."[28]

World War II brought more violations of civil liberties. In 1941, Japan attacked the United States. The U.S. government was afraid that anyone of Japanese heritage living in the United States would spy on the government. The U.S. military forced approximately 120,000 Japanese-Americans out of their homes and sent them to prison camps. President Franklin Roosevelt had signed an executive order that allowed this to happen. "The imprisonment of almost all of the country's citizens of Japanese ancestry, which occurred without a single documented case of treasonable conduct by a Japanese-American, is one of the worst civil liberties abuses in American history,"[29] wrote Christopher Finan, president of the American Booksellers Foundation for Free Expression. Toward the end of the war, the Supreme Court ruled that detaining loyal citizens violated the Constitution. In 1945, the camps were closed. More than 40 years later, the government apologized to those who were interned.

During World War II, people were suspicious of anyone who looked Japanese. This sign was put up by the Japanese-American owner of a grocery store.

Just a few years after World War II, the government violated civil liberties during another "Red Scare." The Cold War had started. This was a standoff between the United States and the Soviet Union, which included what is now known as Russia. Because Russia was a Communist country, members of the Communist Party in the United States were victimized for their beliefs. U.S. Senator Joseph McCarthy conducted hearings and persecuted people suspected of being Communists. People lost their jobs and were even imprisoned because of their political beliefs. The harassment became known as McCarthyism. People accused of being Communists took their cases to court. In most cases, the courts found the government's actions unconstitutional. McCarthy was later criticized for his actions.

Terrorism and Security

On September 11, 2001, al-Qaeda, an Islamic terrorist group, flew two passenger airliners into the World Trade Center in New York City. They also brought down a plane in Pennsylvania and crashed another into the Pentagon in Washington, D.C. The extremist terrorists killed thousands of innocent people.

After the terrorist attacks of September 11, 2001, the government passed laws that many people believed were a violation of civil liberties.

Following the attacks, the U.S. government wanted broader powers to avoid future attacks. Government leaders said they needed to be able to more easily investigate a suspected terrorist. They wanted laws that allowed them to use today's technology, such as cell phones and the Internet, to investigate suspected terrorists. Government agencies that gathered information about people needed to be able to easily share this information, and they also wanted greater access to people's personal records.

President George W. Bush and other politicians developed the Uniting and Strengthening America by Providing Appropriate Tools Required to Intercept and Obstruct Terrorism Act of 2001. Because the name of the act is an acronym for USA PATRIOT, most people simply call it the Patriot Act. It gives the government more power over national security issues. Many groups, such as the ACLU, argued that the expanded powers would allow the government to invade people's privacy, violate the right to free expression, and restrict due process. Despite these objections, Congress passed the Patriot Act 45 days after the September 11 attacks. Elected officials said that the act was necessary to keep U.S. citizens safe and to catch terrorists before they could attack the country again.

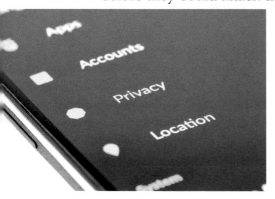

In today's technological world, many people worry about how to keep their personal data safe from the government as well as hackers.

The Patriot Act expanded the government's power to monitor people's activities and records in order to investigate potential terrorists or terrorist activities. For example, the Patriot Act allows federal investigators to get "roving" wiretaps. Once authorities get a warrant for a roving wiretap, they can use it to monitor a suspect's home telephone, cell phone, or computer. Previously, officials needed separate authorization for each device. The Patriot Act also makes it easier for the government to obtain a person's medical, library, financial, student, or mental health records. With the Patriot Act, investigators can look at these records just by saying it is necessary for national security, and they do not have to inform the target of the search.

Citizens Under Surveillance

The Patriot Act allows the government to access a person's personal records held by a third party with relative ease. Many third-party record holders have resisted such actions. For example, Bear Pond Books in Montpelier, Vermont, let its customers know that it would get rid of their buying records if they asked. It also threw away the names of books bought by its readers' club. "When the CIA comes and asks what you've read because they're suspicious of you, we can't tell them because we don't have it," store co-owner Michael Katzenberg said. "That's just a basic right, to be able to read what you want without fear that somebody is looking over your shoulder to see what you're reading."[1]

1 Quoted in Jarrett Murphy, "Bookstores Buck Patriot Act," CBS News, February 21, 2003. www.cbsnews.com/stories/2003/02/21/national/main541464.shtml.

The Patriot Act also strengthened the ways investigators can deal with terrorist activity involving money. Money laundering is how criminals or terrorists move money without detection and then use the money to help them commit their crimes. The Patriot Act improved the government's ability to detect money laundering by requiring banks to monitor the flow of large sums of money and report any suspicious activity to the Department of the Treasury.

Protests to the Patriot Act

Many people agree that the Patriot Act was needed. It updated laws so that government agencies could fight terrorism with today's technology. It also allowed for better communication between governmental agencies and tightened airport security. However, there are many parts of the act that people did not agree with and still do not.

One of the most controversial aspects of the Patriot Act is that it allows so-called "sneak-and-peek" surveillance. If it gets a search warrant, the Federal Bureau of Investigation (FBI) can search a person's house or business without giving him or her immediate notice. Later, after the search, the FBI will give the person the warrant. The Justice Department says that providing notice may jeopardize an investigation. With notice, those investigated may be able to conceal evidence of terrorist activity. Critics say that investigators already had the power to do secret searches in counterterror and counterespionage probes. The problem with this part of the Patriot Act, critics contend, is that it authorizes the use of secret searches for any crime, no matter how minor. This violates people's right to privacy. In 2005, the government confirmed that only 12 percent of sneak-and-peek warrants were related to terrorism; most were actually for drug-related issues.

The Patriot Act also lets the government review people's personal records, even if they are not suspected of a crime. These include health, financial, purchasing, and other records. In the past, a government investigator had to get a warrant to get this information. To get the warrant, the investigator had to go to

Which Groups Do Americans Believe It Is Acceptable for the Government to Monitor?

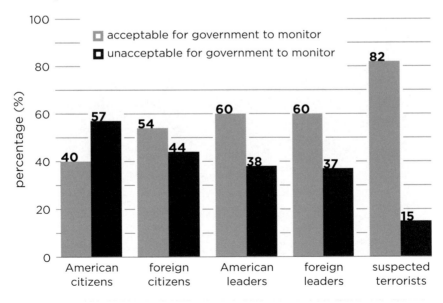

Americans' views on government surveillance vary depending on which group is being monitored, as this information from the Pew Research Center shows.

a federal judge and prove that there was probable cause that a crime had been committed. Now the official can just go to the Foreign Intelligence Surveillance Act (FISA) court and say that the search involves protecting the country against terrorism. The official does not need to make a case for probable cause. The court gives the investigator a subpoena, which requires the record holder, such as a cell phone company or a bank, to hand over the records. Additionally, the subject of the search does not have to be notified that his or her records are being reviewed.

GOVERNMENT WATCH

"The objective of the Patriot Act [is to make] the population visible and the Justice Department invisible. The Act inverts the constitutional requirement that people's lives be private and the work of government officials be public; it instead crafts a set of conditions that make our inner lives transparent and the workings of government opaque."
—Elaine Scarry, professor of English and American literature at Harvard University

Elaine Scarry, "Acts of Resistance," *Harper's Magazine*, May 2004. www.harpers.org/archive/2004/05/0080017

A 2005 CBS poll found that 45 percent of Americans felt the Patriot Act went too far and threatened civil liberties. Some revisions were made in 2006 when the law was renewed; one change allows subpoena recipients to challenge the order not to discuss the case publicly, although they have to wait one year to do so. Another prevents the FBI "from demanding the names of lawyers consulted by people who receive secret government requests for information, and [prevents] most libraries from being subject to requests for records."[30]

Even after the 2006 revisions, Americans have continued to challenge the Patriot Act. Brandon Mayfield was arrested and jailed for two weeks in 2004 when the FBI mistakenly linked him to a terrorist attack in Spain. The FBI secretly searched Mayfield's house and law office, copied his computer files and photos, listened to his telephone conversations, and placed surveillance bugs in his office. The FBI did all of this using warrants issued by FISA. After it realized its mistake, the government apologized and compensated Mayfield. He still decided to take his case to court because he wanted to test the constitutionality of the Patriot Act. In 2007, district judge Ann Aiken ruled that parts of the Patriot Act violate the Constitution because each of those parts "permits the executive branch of government to conduct surveillance and searches of American citizens without satisfying the probable cause requirements of the Fourth Amendment."[31] Still, in 2011, 42 percent of Americans said the Patriot Act was a necessary tool, and only 32 percent said the Patriot Act was a threat to civil liberties. Over time, however, these views changed. According to the Pew Research Center, by 2014, 74 percent of Americans said they did not believe it was necessary to give up privacy and freedom for the sake of safety.

Views on the Patriot Act

Poll of American Citizens, January 2006 and February 2011

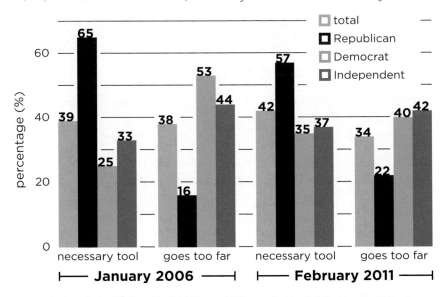

This information from the Pew Research Center shows that Americans' views on the Patriot Act have changed over time.

Prism and National Security

Under the Patriot Act, the National Security Agency (NSA) was able to monitor U.S. citizens without their knowledge. In 2013, a worker inside the NSA named Edward Snowden stole information about the data being collected. He exposed a program called Prism that allowed the NSA to request telephone records of millions of Americans. No one knew their information was being collected until Snowden leaked the information to the media.

Edward Snowden, shown here, was considered a hero by some and a traitor by others after he exposed the Prism program.

The information also showed that the U.S. government was spying on other nations and gathering data. The leak showed information collected on the heads of different countries, including allies of the United States. Foreign governments demanded an end to the data collection. Snowden was charged with stealing information. As of 2017, he is hiding from prosecution in Russia.

SACRIFICING CIVIL LIBERTIES FOR SAFETY

"It may be that by watching everywhere we go, by watching everything we do, by analysing every word we say, by waiting and passing judgment over every association we make and every person we love, that we could uncover a terrorist plot, or we could discover more criminals. But is that the kind of society we want to live in?"
—Edward Snowden, former NSA agent

Quoted in Alan Rusbridger and Ewen MacAskill, "I, Spy: Edward Snowden in Exile," *The Guardian*, July 19, 2014. www.theguardian.com/world/2014/jul/18/-sp-edward-snowden-interview-rusbridger-macaskill.

Updating the Patriot Act

After an extension in 2006, the Patriot Act was set to expire in 2015. Some parts of the law did expire and then were reissued under a new law. The USA Freedom Act was enacted by Congress on June 2, 2015. During the discussion in the Senate, Senator Rand Paul commented, "This is a debate over the bill of rights, over the Fourth Amendment ... It is a debate over your right to be left alone."[32] The USA Freedom Act upholds many of the same provisions as the Patriot Act, but with some modifications. The leak of information by Edward Snowden caused Congress to alter the way the NSA could collect information. Phone records are now held by telephone companies instead of bulk collection by the NSA. The government must ask telephone companies for these records, and the companies have the option to deny a request in court. The USA Freedom Act did restore the ability of the government to use roving wire-tapping, a practice many people object to. Even if a person changes phone numbers, the government can still collect their phone information and listen in.

THE GOVERNMENT'S RIGHT

"Perhaps it offends some sense of privacy if the government is able to obtain records about us held by third parties, such as credit card companies, banks, and businesses. But we have no general constitutional right to privacy over such documents because they are not in our possession."
–John C. Yoo, professor of law at the University of California, Berkeley, and member of the U.S. Justice Department Council

John C. Yoo, "Is the Patriot Act Unconstitutional?," MSN. encarta.msn.com/sidebar_701713501/Is_the_Patriot_Act_Unconstitutional_.html.

Rights During War

In the same year the Patriot Act was passed, the U.S. government took other actions that limited people's rights. These actions affected prisoners of war (POWs). The Bush administration decided that the Geneva Conventions, which the United States signed in 1949, did not protect all Afghan and Iraqi prisoners of war.

The Geneva Conventions are international agreements on how to treat POWs. Countries that sign the Geneva Conventions agree to treat prisoners humanely and according to rules laid out in the document. One requirement is that countries respect prisoners' religions. The agreements do not permit any degrading treatment. Up until 2001, the United States followed these conventions with all POWs.

In 2001, the United States went to war in Afghanistan. The Bush administration stated that the Geneva Conventions did not apply to POWs from Afghanistan. The reason, it said, was because these prisoners were not soldiers from Afghanistan's military. Instead, they were part of a rogue militia, the Taliban, and a terrorist group, al-Qaeda. These prisoners were termed unlawful combatants. As unlawful combatants, these POWs had few rights, so the United States justified torturing them to obtain information.

Some people believed that the government's actions were necessary to deal with potential terrorists. They felt the U.S. government needed more freedom when questioning prisoners who may have been involved in terrorism. Others argued that this abused civil liberties. They contended that all people, no matter what they have done, have natural rights. These include the right not to be tortured and the right to be represented in a court. Additionally, they feared that many innocent men and foot soldiers might be captured and treated the same as hardened terrorists.

Without the Geneva Conventions, the prisoners had no clear rights. This issue caused disagreement even within the Bush administration. Secretary of State Colin Powell was among the critics. In a memo, he wrote that the decision to ignore the Geneva Conventions would "reverse over a century of U.S. policy and practice and undermine the protections of the law of war for our troops."[33]

Some believe that President Bush's decision led to civil rights abuses. These critics claim that by denying some prisoners Geneva Conventions, the government set a tone that the rights of all POWs could be ignored. The International Committee of the Red Cross found that the U.S. military had tortured prisoners

When Civil Liberties Are Suspended

Some U.S. soldiers stationed at Abu Ghraib in Iraq tortured POWs. Pictures, interviews, and even films document this. "The U.S., which was viewed as certainly one of the principal advocates of human rights and the dignity of human beings in the world, suddenly is viewed as a principal expositor of torture,"[1] said Scott Horton, the chairman of the Committee on International Law of the New York City Bar Association. Some critics claim that U.S. government policies made Abu Ghraib possible. Many military personnel who were stationed at Abu Ghraib said the prisoner abuses were part of a general pattern of a "gloves off" interrogation policy. They said the United States put this policy into place after 9/11. The White House claimed that what happened at Abu Ghraib was an unacceptable occurrence. It said the abuses were the fault of on-site leadership. However, investigations showed that torture orders may have come from high-ranking government officials. After many investigations, 11 low-ranking soldiers received court-martials. Only one high-ranking officer was penalized.

Prisoners of war were tortured by U.S. soldiers at Abu Ghraib even though the United States had signed the Geneva Conventions.

1. Quoted in "Ghosts of Abu Ghraib," HBO. www.hbo.com/docs/programs/ghostsofabughraib/synopsis.html.

at the Abu Ghraib prison in Iraq. These prisoners were supposed to be protected by the Geneva Conventions. Instead, they were physically and mentally abused. According to a Red Cross report, military intelligence officers estimate that somewhere between 70 and 90 percent of those whom they detained were picked up by mistake and were not guilty of any crime.

Guantánamo Bay Abuses

Many prisoners were held at the detention center at the U.S. Guantánamo Bay Naval Base in Cuba. Critics believed detainees were kept away from the U.S. mainland to limit their ability to be heard in court. The Bush administration said terror suspects did not have the right to come into U.S. courts and demand the rights that U.S. citizens have under the legal system. Instead, the U.S. government said that the suspects would receive justice through military tribunals. The government declared them "enemy combatants" in order to deny them the civil liberties POWs have.

UNDERMINING CIVIL LIBERTIES

"The continued operation of the Guantanamo facility damages U.S. diplomatic relations and our standing in the world. It undermines America's indispensable leadership on human rights and other critical foreign policy and national security matters. In particular, the Guantanamo detention facility consistently impedes joint counterterrorism efforts with friends and allies."
—John Kerry, former secretary of state

John Kerry, letter to the Committee on Foreign Relations, Scribd, November 13, 2013. www.scribd.com/doc/185248726/Kerry-letter-on-GTMO-NDAA-November-2013.

U.S. courts ruled that the detainees were denied their right to due process. In 2006, the U.S. Supreme Court ruled that the president was out of line when he ordered military war crimes trials for some Guantánamo Bay detainees. The court majority opinion stated that holding military trials for foreign terror suspects was illegal under U.S. law and the Geneva Conventions without congressional approval. The court ruled that U.S.

federal courts could hear appeals from enemy combatants in U.S. military custody. Since then, more cases have gone to court. In 2008, a federal judge ordered the release of five detainees because the government failed to prove they were enemy combatants. The five men had been held at Guantánamo for more than six years.

Some prisoners are held illegally for years. Even if they are eventually released, they will never get that time back.

From 2001 to 2008, 775 detainees were brought to Guantánamo. By 2016, all but 61 were released without charge. Only one prisoner was actually convicted of a crime. President Barack Obama declared that he would close the prison at Guantánamo Bay during his presidency, but he was unable to accomplish this during his two terms in office.

Keeping a country both safe and free is not easy. The U.S. government needs to protect the country to keep it free. At the same time, it may need—or feel it needs—to restrict certain freedoms to do so. Finding a balance is difficult and will continue to be a challenge in the future.

CHAPTER 5

Special Population Issues

Although the Constitution grants civil liberties to all people, many groups have needed to fight for their rights over the course of history. African Americans, women, and immigrants have had an especially difficult struggle. Even now, these groups' rights are often violated. Many people believe that civil rights extend only to citizens, but this is untrue; immigrants, whether documented or undocumented, also have rights guaranteed to them by the Constitution.

African Americans have had to fight for their liberties. Until the mid-19th century, many were slaves to white Americans and did not have any rights at all. In 1865, the 13th Amendment abolished slavery, and former slaves were recognized as citizens. However, discrimination continued. It took years of protests and court cases before the U.S government would protect the natural freedoms of African Americans.

The U.S. government now has laws that protect the rights of all African Americans. People's attitudes have also changed. In 2008 and 2012, U.S. citizens elected Barack Obama, a black man, to be the country's president. However, the election of Obama did not end the struggles of many African Americans. About a quarter of black Americans still live in poverty—nearly three times the rate of white Americans. "A mere election does not change the abject conditions for African Americans or the 230 plus years of racial injustices,"[34] stated Marc Morial, the president and chief executive officer of the National Urban League.

Profiling by Police

Racial profiling is one area of concern for African Americans and others who believe it is regularly practiced by law enforcement. Racial profiling is when a law enforcement officer stops and searches a person because of his or her color, race, or ethnicity, not because the person has broken any laws.

According to studies, including one by the University of Pennsylvania, police are more likely to stop and search cars driven by black people than those driven by whites. Some people believe this is due to police officers being racist. Others claim that police officers do not target race. Instead, they say, the police are pulling over people because of characteristics linked with their race. For example, if statistics show that black drivers are more likely to carry illegal drugs, then racial profiling supporters believe it is acceptable to pull over more black drivers.

Critics argue that it does not matter what statistics show. They say racial profiling violates people's constitutional rights. The Fourth Amendment guarantees people in the United States the right to be safe from unreasonable searches and seizures without probable cause. Being of a certain race, critics argue, does not give a police officer probable cause. Additionally, critics cite the 14th Amendment. This requires that all citizens be treated equally under the law. Subjecting a person to a search because of his or her race violates this amendment.

An Unequal Policing

Some state laws allow police to stop pedestrians and ask questions or even search them for weapons or drugs. These laws are called Terry Laws after a Supreme Court case, *Terry v. Ohio*. The Supreme Court ruled in this 1968 case that a police officer could search someone if they had probable cause, which means the police officer must believe a person has committed, is committing, or is about to commit a crime. The Fourth Amendment to the Constitution protects people from illegal searches, but the court ruled that a reasonable suspicion was not a violation of the Fourth Amendment.

The city of New York called its Terry Laws "stop-and-frisk." The stop-and-frisk program started in the 1990s and resulted in millions of citizens being stopped and searched over the years. Over half a million people were stopped in 2011. Of these stops, 88 percent resulted in no convictions for crimes. Most of the citizens stopped in New York City were black or Latinx. Many people complained that people of color were unfairly targeted by stop-and-frisk.

In 2013, civil rights activist Jesse Jackson, shown here, participated in a protest against New York City's stop-and-frisk policy.

New York City police officer Adrian Schoolcraft began to document the program in one neighborhood. His data showed that black people were being unfairly stopped by police. With this information, the courts in New York began to look into stop-and-frisk. On August 12, 2013, U.S. District Court Judge Shira A. Scheindlin ruled the program unconstitutional. She upheld the Terry Laws but said the way they were practiced in New York City unfairly targeted minorities. She called for the police to overhaul the program under the guidance of an outside lawyer. By 2015, the number of people stopped by the New York City police had dropped from half a million to 22,929.

Civil Liberties for the Disabled

Disabled people often deal with unfair treatment. One example is that they have been kept from jobs because of their disabilities. Another is that public transportation and public places do not always accommodate their needs. In 1990, in an attempt to make things fairer for people with disabilities, Congress passed the Americans with Disabilities Act (ADA). The ADA prohibits disability discrimination in employment, public services, public accommodations, and telecommunications. It was amended in 2008 to broaden the definition of a disability. This means that more people are covered under the law. The ADA is an example of what can be done when a group works together to defend their civil liberties. The ADA passed because more than 100 groups dedicated to disability rights, civil rights, and social justice worked together.

Arresting someone without probable cause is a violation of civil liberties. However, Raymond Hall, a black electrician, believes it is a typical occurrence among African Americans. Hall was arrested when he was returning home after getting gas. Two officers ordered him to step out of his car. According to Hall, when he asked why, the officers arrested him at gunpoint. "It's just a common thing," Hall said. "You see it all the time in the neighborhood. They pull you over, ask you a lot of questions. Sometimes they let you go, sometimes they don't."[35] The officer wrote in his report that he stopped Hall because his car was missing a front license plate and a driver's side mirror. He arrested Hall for obstruction when Hall did not turn off his cell phone. When Hall turned up in court to fight the obstruction charge, prosecutors did not press charges; they cited that there were issues with proof, and the case was dropped.

Equal Treatment Under the Law

Affirmative action is another civil liberties issue important to many Americans. For years, employers and schools denied equal opportunities to African Americans and other people of color. Affirmative action programs were created to open up schools and workplaces to everyone, regardless of race. The programs specifically recruit people from minority groups. Some of the programs give minority applicants preferential treatment. They may not have to meet the same standards as other candidates.

Preferential treatment makes affirmative action a hot topic. Opponents of affirmative action say it is unfair. They claim that a person who is offered a job or admission to a school because of his or her race is given an unequal advantage. Although some critics do agree that affirmative action was initially needed to get companies and schools to open their doors, they think it is no longer needed because people have equal opportunities.

Shown here are students protesting against a court case that could limit affirmative action practices for college admissions.

Some courts agree with this view. The U.S. Court of Appeals struck down a government program that gave minority contractors special treatment. The government's defense program set aside 5 percent of its contract work for companies run by minorities. Because of this program, minority-owned companies received $15 billion of defense contracts in 2006. In 2008, the court decided that this program was unfair.

Many people argue that affirmative action is still needed to correct past wrongs. They also believe that discrimination still happens at companies and schools. Without affirmative action, people of color may lose opportunities. In her dissent after a court ruling on affirmative action in Michigan Universities in

2014, Supreme Court Justice Sonia Sotomayor provided support for affirmative action: "The way to stop discrimination on the basis of race is to speak openly and candidly on the subject of race, and to apply the Constitution with eyes open to the unfortunate effects of centuries of racial discrimination."[36] Justice Sotomayor and others agree that affirmative action can help minorities overcome discrimination.

Second-Class Rights

Women have also faced discrimination, and women of color have faced even more discrimination than white women. They have struggled to be treated equally by employers, governments, schools, companies, and individuals. Laws have kept them from owning property, from having fair representation in court, and from other basic freedoms.

In many countries, women have made great strides. Many countries have adopted laws that allow women to vote and serve in the government. Laws have been instituted that guarantee women equal opportunity in employment and education. In countries such as the United States, those in the European Union, and more, women have the same legal status as men.

In spite of these achievements, women still face discrimination in the United States and abroad due to their sex. Some countries have even more limited rights for women, seeing them as second-class citizens. Their right to control their own lives is limited by culture and the law. In Saudi Arabia, women are not allowed to drive a vehicle or ride a bike on public roads in big cities. In Iran, girls can be legally forced to marry at age 13. In both countries, a woman's legal testimony is worth less than a man's, which makes it difficult for a woman to prove that her rights have been violated.

In countries where women are seen as inferior, the laws do not protect their basic rights. For example, over 270 young girls were taken from their school in Nigeria in 2015. The girls were abducted by a group called Boko Haram, which then sold them into slavery. Boko Haram does not believe women should be educated. Since then, a few of the girls have been rescued and returned to their homes. Unfortunately, since women are still considered property, many were rejected from their families because they had been raped and were therefore considered less valuable. These girls, who only wanted an education, now have no home or family to support them.

In 2014, African women's organizations held a march demanding the return of the schoolgirls Boko Haram had kidnapped.

Property for Women

Another global civil liberties issue for women is property rights. In many developing countries, women's natural property rights are routinely violated. Cultural norms or laws bar women from owning a house or land. In Syria, for example, the government officially protects women's property rights. However, many local communities apply traditional custom rather than the law. They follow the Islamic tradition for inheritance, which grants women only half the share received by men. Following the death of a parent, a son receives twice the amount that his sister gets. A wife inherits just one-quarter of her dead husband's property if there are no children and one-eighth if there are children. In contrast, a husband gets half or a quarter of his late wife's assets. As a result, many women become impoverished after the death of a husband.

Governments around the world try to help women in developing countries. In the United States, the Office of International Women's Issues works to advance global women's causes. The office makes sure that women's rights are part of U.S. foreign aid programs. For example, in 2011 alone, the United States provided over $28 million in grants for Afghan women and children.

BASIC RIGHTS FOR WOMEN

"The rights we want: We want to choose our husband, we want to own the land, we want to go to school, we don't want to be cut anymore, we want also to make decisions, we want respect in politics, to be leaders, we want to be equal."
—Rebecca Lolosoli, activist for women's rights in Kenya

Quoted in Mary Scharffenberger and Anna Lemberger, "14 Inspirational Quotes from Pioneering Women," One.org, March 4, 2015. www.one.org/us/2015/03/04/14-inspirational-quotes-from-pioneering-women/.

Women Serving in Wartime

In countries where women have more freedom, equal opportunity in the workplace, particularly in the military, is still an issue. In developed countries, women can serve in the military. However, they are limited from certain combat jobs. Many military women believe that all military jobs should be open to them if they are physically and mentally capable. Others disagree. They argue that serving in combat is bad for women, their families, and the people serving with them.

Despite the controversy, women's combat roles, particularly in the United States, have increased. When they first were allowed in the military, American women were excluded from all combat. In the early 1990s, Congress lifted the ban on women flying combat aircraft and serving on combat ships, but women were still excluded from certain combat positions. The Pentagon did not allow women to serve in ground combat units at the front lines.

In 2015, Secretary of Defense Ashton B. Carter declared all combat roles open to women. He declared, "There will be no exceptions. They'll be allowed to drive tanks, fire mortars and lead infantry soldiers into combat. They'll be able to serve as Army Rangers and Green Berets, Navy SEALs, Marine Corps infantry, Air Force parajumpers and everything else that was previously open only to men."[37] The new rule went into effect in 2016.

WOMEN'S ROLE IN WAR

"Women are citizens. And when they volunteer, we ought to be able to let them to use all their abilities to defend this country, not sequester them and put an extra burden on the men who are over there."
—Lory Manning, U.S. Navy captain and the director of the Women's Research and Education Institution in Washington, D.C.

Quoted in "Women In War: Should They Be In the Frontlines?," MSNBC, 2009. www.msnbc.msn.com/id/8407338/.

Opponents of this move believe that having women in combat roles will hurt morale. They say these restrictions are also needed because women are not strong enough to perform the tasks needed in combat. However, this has been definitively proven false. Ranger School is known to be so difficult that not everyone can complete it, but in 2015, two women completed the school. Captain Kristen M. Griest, one of the two women, later went on to become the first woman officer in an infantry unit, which was opened to women with Secretary Carter's ruling. Captain Griest helped prove women were just as capable in combat roles as men.

The Iraq War may have inadvertently opened up more combat roles for women. From 2002 to 2007, women served nearly 170,000 tours of duty in Iraq and Afghanistan. Although they did not serve in ground combat units, they served in support

Captain Kristen Griest (left) and First Lieutenant Shaye Haver (right) were the first two women to complete Ranger School.

units as truck drivers, gunners, medics, military police, helicopter pilots, and more. Because there is no official front line, even support units ended up serving at the front. Many women believe their service in the line of fire proved that all areas of the military should be open to women if they are qualified. Army captain Andrea So believes that combat in Iraq has taught military men that women are equally capable to serve. "Guys saw that their female counterparts could really handle themselves,"[38] said So of her Iraq tour.

The Right to Love Anyone

Like women and people of color, gay men and women also have been subjected to violations of their civil liberties. In some countries, it is still illegal to be gay, and gay men and women have often been the targets of violence. For instance, in 2017, reports surfaced of human rights violations in Chechnya—gay men were being hunted down and killed, tortured, or held against their will at detention centers. In other countries, gay people have gained more protection of their inherent rights. However, even in these countries, the question of gay rights is hotly debated.

Whether gay marriage should be allowed is still debated throughout the United States despite a Supreme Court ruling nationally legalizing gay marriage. Until the Supreme Court

Rights of Students in the Digital Age

In a 1965 case called *Tinker v. Des Moines*, the Supreme Court ruled that students do have freedom of speech in school, but that right and others are restricted; schools have a lot of freedom to decide what statements and actions will interfere with other students' ability to learn. The Supreme Court ruled in its decision that a school "must be able to show that its action was caused by something more than a mere desire to avoid the discomfort and unpleasantness that always accompany an unpopular viewpoint,"[1] but some students believe that schools regularly overstep this boundary.

With the rise of the Internet, free speech in schools has become more complicated, and students are sometimes punished for things they post online outside of school hours. According to *The Atlantic*,

In 2012, after a Minnesota student wrote a Facebook post saying a hall monitor was "mean" to her, she was forced to turn over her Facebook password to school administrators—in the presence of a sheriff's deputy. The school made an out-of-court settlement with the student, who was represented by the ACLU.[2]

Some schools have made rules prohibiting students from posting anything mean or intimidating online, whether they do so in school or at home. Some people support these rules, saying that they protect students and teachers from online bullies. Others oppose them because they fear schools will be able to punish students who make any statement they do not agree with as long as they can claim the post was intimidating. Dozens of cases regarding students' right to free speech have gone to court in the last decade and will likely continue to do so in the future.

1. Quoted in David R. Wheeler, "Do Students Still Have Free Speech in School?," *The Atlantic*, April 7, 2014. www.theatlantic.com/education/archive/2014/04/do-students-still-have-free-speech-in-school/360266/
2. Wheeler, "Do Students Still Have Free Speech in School?"

ruling, only a few states gave gay people the right to marry. Some Americans believed that homosexual relationships were not protected civil liberties. "A marriage and a homosexual relationship are two different kinds of relationships and it is a misuse of civil rights law to use that law to try to blot out the difference between two different kinds of things,"[39] wrote James Skillen of the Center for Public Justice.

The Supreme Court disagreed. In the 2015 case *Obergefell v. Hodges*, the court ruled that homosexual couples have the same rights as heterosexual couples. Justice Anthony Kennedy gave the ruling. It read in part:

It would misunderstand these men and women to say they disrespect the idea of marriage. Their plea is that they do respect it, respect it so deeply that they seek to find its fulfillment for themselves. Their hope is not to be condemned to live in loneliness, excluded from one of civilization's oldest institutions. They ask for equal dignity in the eyes of the law. The Constitution grants them that right.[40]

Same-sex marriage supporters celebrated after the Supreme Court ruled in 2015 that individual states could no longer ban same-sex marriage.

Another major issue is whether gay people should be allowed to adopt children. As with marriage, gay people argue that denying them the right to adopt children violates their civil liberties. Some state governments agree, but others disagree. In 2008, a Florida circuit court struck down a state law that barred gay men and women from adopting. Within eight years, a judge struck down the last ban on gay adoption. The state of Mississippi was the last to ban gay men and women from adopting.

The judge cited the ruling that all marriages were now equal after the Supreme Court ruling on same-sex marriage.

Supporters of gay adoption argue that, in addition to denying gay people's rights, restricting gay men and women from adopting denies children the right to security. "The United States has many children waiting to be adopted. Older children and those with special needs are especially hard to place," wrote Kathy Belge, a lesbian activist. "Children who fit this category are in foster homes right now with gay and lesbian parents who want to adopt them. It is unfair to the children to deny them permanent secure homes."[41]

In 2016, same-sex parents were raising 65,000 adopted children in the United States. This accounts for 4 percent of all adoptions. One or more gay foster parents were caring for an additional 14,100 foster children, making up 3 percent of foster children. Some states still have laws that prohibit gay couples from fostering children.

Undocumented Immigrants

Worldwide, undocumented immigrants grapple with civil liberties. One major debate is what government services countries should provide to these immigrants. Some people say that health care is a right and governments should provide health care to anyone who cannot afford it, including undocumented immigrants. Others argue that getting free health care is a benefit of citizenship, not a right. To them, undocumented immigrants do not have a legal right to be in the country, so they should not get its benefits.

Countries take different viewpoints about this matter. France denies health care to undocumented immigrants. Sweden and the United States federally fund only emergency health care for undocumented immigrants. Even countries with specific policies are not clear about how to deal with every issue. In the United States, all hospitals must treat and stabilize a patient even if they cannot pay. This law means that many undocumented people receive life-saving treatment. Most of the emergency care given to undocumented immigrants is for childbirth.

The Patient Protection and Affordable Care Act of 2010 stated that in order to receive health care outside of an emergency, people must prove their citizenship. This means undocumented immigrants cannot purchase health care or be covered by federal programs such as Medicaid and Medicare. Only U.S. citizens can access health care.

DREAMers

"[The DREAM Act] says that if your parents brought you here as a child, if you've been here for five years, and you're willing to go to college or serve in our military, you can one day earn your citizenship." —Barack Obama, 44th president of the United States

Barack Obama, "Remarks by the President on Immigration," the White House, June 15, 2012. www.whitehouse.gov/the-press-office/2012/06/15/remarks-president-immigration.

Another debate is about what the government should provide to children of undocumented immigrants. For example, is education a right? In many countries, including the United States, the answer is yes. In 1982, the U.S. Supreme Court struck down a 1975 Texas law that denied free public education to school-age children of undocumented immigrants. Now children of undocumented immigrants across the country can enroll in public schools.

Immigration, Border Protection, and Civil Liberties

Shortly after taking office in 2017, President Donald Trump signed a number of executive orders—laws the president can sign without the approval of Congress. Executive orders are directions to the executive branch of the government. Every department of the U.S. government belongs to the executive branch. Some of these include the Department of State, the Department of Homeland Security, and the Department of Justice. Executive orders are official once they are signed by the president. They then become law, and departments must change or adapt their own rules to follow.

On January 27, 2017, President Trump signed an executive order entitled "Protecting the Nation from Foreign Terrorist Entry into the United States." The order started by mentioning the September 11, 2001, terrorist attacks on New York, Washington, D.C., and Pennsylvania. Even though security had been tightened already under the Patriot Act and the USA Freedom Act, this new executive order intended to further restrict immigration. Part of the order included a 90-day restriction preventing citizens of certain countries from entering the country, stating that these foreign citizens would "be detrimental to the interests of the United States."[42] These countries were predominantly Muslim and included Iran, Iraq, Sudan, Yemen, Somalia, and Syria.

Anyone who enters the United States must first pass through Customs. Agents are stationed at airports, train stations, and other borders of the United States. The Customs agents look at passports and visas to determine if someone has a right to enter the United States. Following the 2017 executive order, agents began rejecting citizens of the countries specified in the order. This meant that these men and women were either not allowed to board their plane to the United States or were not allowed through airport security when they arrived in the country. Many were booked on a flight back to the country they had come from. Some foreign citizens were held in airports around the United States overnight and questioned by Customs agents and police. They included families whose children were handcuffed while waiting for Customs to tell them if they could enter the United States.

The order also stated that the "Secretary of State shall suspend the U.S. Refugee Admissions Program (USRAP) for 120 days."[43] Trump specifically included language about Syrian refugees. Syria has been fighting a civil war, which has caused a refugee crisis as millions of families and individuals flee the fighting. As of 2016, the United States had committed to taking in 10,000 of the millions of displaced Syrians. With this executive order, even Syrians who had passed the extensive refugee background checks were now banned from the United States. This included Syrian children coming to the United States for quality medical care. In response, other countries such as Canada began to accept these children and provide medical care.

In response to the executive order, immigration lawyers across the country went to airports to work for free. The lawyers wanted to ensure that the civil liberties of each foreign national were not being denied. The day after the order was signed, the ACLU and other civil liberties groups sued President Trump and the Department of Homeland Security, which oversees Customs, to stop the ban. The ACLU's case was based on the experience of two men from Iraq. One of the men, Hameed Khalid Darweesh, had served as an interpreter for the U.S. Army in Iraq. Iraqi citizens who helped the army were often targeted for murder by terrorist groups. After extensive background checks, Darweesh had been granted permission to enter the United States. However, because of the executive order, he was stopped at JFK Airport in New York City and denied entry to the United States.

On February 3, U.S. District Court Senior Judge James L. Robart from the state of Washington granted the ACLU's request for a stop to the executive order. This court agreement did not erase the ban; it temporarily stopped the enforcement of the ban. Some agencies under the Department of Homeland Security did not initially follow the court order, saying that the original ban had erased visas and anyone who had been denied entry since January 27 would have to reapply for a visa. On February 4, the Department of State said that these previously denied visa holders would now be accepted without having to reapply. The president voiced his disappointment with the court order on Twitter. The ACLU and other lawyers continued to provide support for foreign nationals.

On February 7, the Department of Justice brought the executive order to an appellate court—a court that hears appeals to decisions made by other judges. A three-judge panel from the U.S. Court of Appeals for the 9th Circuit in San Francisco, California, heard arguments on whether to keep the executive order or permanently stop it. The court ultimately made the decision not to reinstate the order. It will continue to be debated in court, but while that is happening, it will not be enforced.

The issues that immigrants face have been ongoing for years and will continue to be debated, along with the many issues women and people of color face, particularly as traditional ideas are challenged and questions of equal rights versus special treatment are discussed.

CHAPTER 9

A Right to Privacy

The right to privacy means people have the right to make personal decisions without government interference. Parents are able to choose what TV shows their children can watch, people can decide where to travel, and no one is forced to eat certain foods. The right to privacy also protects people's personal documents, records, and property from the government.

Most European countries protect privacy. The European Convention on Human Rights guarantees that a person's family life, home, and correspondence should be free from interference. The European Union requires all of its member states to have laws that protect their citizens' right to privacy. The United States also protects the right to privacy in many cases. This right is not explicitly stated in the Bill of Rights. However, the U.S. Supreme Court has interpreted privacy rights in the First, Fourth, and Fifth Amendments. The Supreme Court has ruled that most personal decisions are private and the government cannot interfere with these.

The right to privacy is protected in the Universal Declaration of Human Rights, the document created by the United Nations.

79

Some countries, such as Zimbabwe, do not protect the right to privacy. Although Zimbabwe's constitution states that it protects privacy, its laws conflict with this statement. In August 2007, the president of Zimbabwe signed into law the Interception of Communications Act. This act gives the government the authority to eavesdrop on people's phone calls and read their mail and e-mail. The country's communication minister can approve the surveillance of people's correspondence without getting court approval. Basically, the government has the authority to eavesdrop on anyone for any reason.

When Privacy Meets Morality

Arguments arise about a person's right to privacy when it conflicts with other people's moral beliefs. For example, in some cases, a parent may choose to keep his or her child from getting medical care. This could be for religious or other private reasons. Many people believe this is morally wrong. They believe that an underage child's right to proper treatment outweighs the parent's right to a private decision about medical care.

U.S. courts have ruled differently on such cases depending on the situation. The courts consider the child's age, the family's reason for declining treatment, and whether the treatment has been shown to work. In 1999, the Oregon Supreme Court ruled that a mother could refuse treatment for her HIV-infected four-year-old son. The court ruled this way because it said her refusal was not an imminent threat to her son.

The courts ruled differently in the case of Dale and Leilani Neumann, whose daughter, Madeline, had diabetes. The Neumanns are Christian Scientists who believe that prayer alone heals without medical treatment. Even when their daughter was extremely sick, they would not take her to the hospital. She eventually died from lack of treatment. In 2008, a court in Wisconsin convicted the Neumanns of second-degree reckless homicide.

The right to privacy is a key argument for parents who are against vaccines. Although no reputable study has ever proven that vaccines cause autism, asthma, or other health conditions, some parents believe vaccines pose a health risk to their children. As of 2016, all 50 states require children to be vaccinated before they enter public school to minimize the risk of spreading dangerous diseases. If a child is not vaccinated, he or she must be homeschooled. All states allow exemptions if the child is allergic to a particular vaccine, 47 states allow exemptions based on religious beliefs, and 17 allow philosophical exemptions for parents who do not trust vaccines. Many anti-vaccine parents oppose laws that do not allow them to enroll their unvaccinated child in public school.

Sexual Orientation and Privacy

Sexuality is another privacy issue that sparks moral arguments. Some people believe that homosexuality is wrong. Others argue that homosexuality is natural and a person's sexual choices are private. In 2016, homosexual activity was illegal in more than 70 countries, though the number falls every year.

For many years, states kept anti-homosexuality laws on the books. For example, two men named John Geddes Lawrence and Tyron Garner were arrested because they had sexual intercourse in Texas. In 2003, the Supreme Court heard their case. The Court struck down the Texas law that prohibited homosexual sex. It ruled that people's sexual choices should be private. "The petitioners are entitled to respect for their private lives," Supreme Court Justice Anthony Kennedy wrote in the decision. "The state cannot demean their existence or control their destiny by making their private sexual conduct a crime."[44] Since the 2015 ruling on same-sex marriage, other laws against homosexuality in the United States have also been struck down.

Life and Death

Life and death choices are also considered private choices. However, people's different views on morality make these decisions more complicated. For years, abortion has been a topic that is heatedly, and at times violently, debated. Many people believe a woman has a right to decide whether to have a baby. Pro-choice supporters believe this is a personal, private choice that should not be interfered with by the government. They believe that the right to decide belongs to the pregnant woman.

Pro-life supporters believe the government should step in to protect unborn babies. They believe abortion violates the unborn fetus's right to life, so the government should restrict or ban it.

THE RIGHT TO LIFE

"I believe it's necessary to ensure that there's never a case in the country where a sick or elderly person feels under pressure to agree to an assisted death, or somehow feels it's the expected thing to do."
—Former British Prime Minister Gordon Brown on why he opposes assisted suicide

Quoted in Sarah Lyall, "TV Broadcast of an Assisted Suicide Intensifies a Contentious Debate in Britain," *New York Times*, December 11, 2008. www.nytimes.com/2008/12/11/world/europe/11suicide.html

Around the world, countries hold different views on abortion. In Chile, it is illegal except to save the mother's life. In Poland, lawmakers tried to make abortion illegal in all cases. In 2016, women in Poland held large protests stating that it was not the government's decision. The ban on abortion did not become law. In the United States, abortion has been legal and a private choice since 1973. However, this law is still continually tested and debated.

In addition to right-to-life debates, around the world, there are right-to-die debates. These discussions concern whether it is a person's private choice to die. In these cases, the person who wants to die is generally experiencing chronic and severe physical pain or a life-threatening illness. The person wants to die with a physician's help, usually through a lethal dose of drugs. This is called medical-assisted euthanasia or suicide.

Some countries recognize the right to die as a private decision. Eight countries, including Switzerland, the Netherlands, and Belgium, allow physician-assisted suicide. Only in Switzerland can a noncitizen obtain a physician's help. In the United States, five states—California, Colorado, Oregon, Vermont, and Washington—as well as Washington, D.C., allow assisted suicide. In Montana, it is decided on a case-by-case basis in court.

A RIGHT TO DIE

"But what about for those few whose pain doesn't stop, and who face a lingering death that robs them of all dignity in their final weeks? Don't they deserve the same care we give the family dog and cat?"
–Dotty E. LeMieux, an officer in the California Democratic Party Progressive Caucus

Dotty E. LeMieux, "Time for Compassionate Choice in California," California Progress Report, May 24, 2006. www.californiaprogressreport.com/2006/05/time_for_compas.html.

Brittany Maynard was diagnosed with an aggressive brain tumor in January 2014. She was only given a few months to live. She decided that she wanted to have the choice to end her life before cancer did. Maynard moved to Oregon, which has a "Death with Dignity" law. Maynard became an advocate for the right to die. She wrote and spoke on the subject before her death. In November 2014, she decided to end her life, saying, "I've discussed with many experts how I would die from it and it's a terrible, terrible way to die. So being able to choose to go with dignity is less terrifying."[45] Her family went on to continue speaking and advocating for others to have the right to decide when to die.

Personal Information

Privacy issues extend beyond personal choices. They are also about personal records. Governments, in order to run properly, need to keep certain records about people. They need personal records in order to collect taxes, to issue driver's licenses, and to call people for jury duty. Out of respect for privacy, many governments have laws that make sure the records are not accessed by third parties.

Countries such as the United States, Canada, and Australia have privacy acts to protect personal records held by government agencies. The U.S. Privacy Act became law in 1974. The Electronic Privacy Information Center summarized the act:

First, it requires government agencies to show an individual any records kept on him or her. Second, it requires agencies to follow certain

The security of people's personal information has become a big issue in the 21st century.

principles, called "fair information practices," when gathering and handling personal data. Third, it places restrictions on how agencies can share an individual's data with other people and agencies. Fourth and finally, it lets individuals sue the government for violating its provisions.[46]

Government Collection of Private Information

People in the United States are also concerned about the government gaining access to personal records held by third parties. This concern was heightened after 9/11, when the U.S. government expanded its powers to more easily view people's records without warrants. The information provided by Edward Snowden in the NSA leak confirmed these fears.

In December 2003, for example, the U.S. government received a tip that al-Qaeda might attack Las Vegas, Nevada. The FBI demanded that businesses there provide all records about tourists who visited over the holiday period. Hotels, car rental agencies, casinos, and more had to turn over purchasing records with people's names, their addresses, their phone numbers, what services they paid for, and what dates they used the services.

The city's tourist industry did not want to hand over all the information that the FBI requested. "What we seem to be witnessing at this point is a move on the part of the government to keep tabs on what everyone is doing all the time, which has serious civil liberties implications," said Allen Lichtenstein, the general counsel for the Nevada chapter of the American Civil Liberties Union. "It's one thing to have some specific security concerns and a targeted investigation with some basis in fact, but to … try to follow everyone goes beyond what is called for."[47]

The government issued national security letters that forced the Las Vegas companies to produce the data. The FBI checked

250,000 Las Vegas visitors against terrorist watch lists. No known terrorist suspects or associates of suspects turned up in the check. The FBI said the records it received were destroyed after two years.

Privacy on the Internet

People share a lot of information when using the Internet and cell phones, and much of this information is easily traceable. Third parties, such as ISPs and cell phone companies, store much of this information, and it is easier to sift through electronic data rather than paper records. "Technology makes it easier to keep tabs on millions, even hundreds of millions, of consumers and citizens," wrote David H. Holtzman, the author of *Privacy Lost*. "Not only is the storage of consumers' data cheaper and easier to search than with paper, but also a single person can easily run the whole tracking process."[48]

People are concerned about the security of their personal information, specifically from marketers and the government. They are concerned because, in many countries, no all-encompassing law regulates the acquisition, storage, or use of personal data. In the United States, the government has not wanted to restrict the development of new technology. "Congress, which has trouble grappling with technology issues in general, has been particularly slow in adapting privacy laws to the runaway evolution of the Internet," wrote Joelle Tessler for *Congressional Quarterly*. "The resulting gap between Internet practices and privacy protection has left an increasing amount of personal data on the Internet wide open to government snooping."[49]

Without specific laws, ISPs and other companies can decide what information they collect, what they do with that information, and whether they tell consumers they are collecting it. Many companies sell customer data to third parties for marketing purposes. Some of these companies were taken to court for selling the information but not because they broke a federal law; the companies broke their own privacy policies. Additionally, in the United States and other countries, governments may request information from ISPs as well as companies such as Google and Facebook. In the United States, such a request does not necessarily require a warrant.

Privacy at Work

People are concerned about their privacy at the workplace. When a person sends an e-mail from a work computer, can they expect it to be private? What if someone visits a website while at work? Although the U.S. Privacy Act gives them some protection from government interference, most laws do not cover employer surveillance. In fact, more than 75 percent of U.S. companies have an electronic monitoring system. Employers can read e-mails, listen to phone calls, and monitor employee website visits. Companies are subject to little restriction. If employees use company-owned equipment to conduct personal business, courts have ruled that companies can monitor their use. Some employers—but not all—tell their employees that they are being watched. For now, if people in the United States send e-mails or check websites at work, they should remember that someone could be watching.

Civil liberties generally refer to protection of citizens from their government. Private insitutions, such as businesses, are not required to protect certain rights, such as the right to privacy.

Because of all these issues, countries are now updating privacy laws to include today's technology. They are beginning to institute laws that regulate what ISPs, website hosts, and cell phone providers can do with their customer information. The United Kingdom, Switzerland, and many other European countries have adopted data protection acts. These acts detail what can and cannot be done with people's information. For example, the United Kingdom's act states that data must not be disclosed to other parties without the consent of the individual involved.

The Government and Data Privacy

Because there are few U.S. laws that protect data privacy, people are concerned that the government will access their cell phone and Internet records. This concern is not unfounded. For example, the Justice Department has interpreted existing phone wiretap laws to also mean it can track people's e-mails and websites. "The government is acquiring far more surveillance powers as a result of the digital revolution,"[50] stated James Dempsey of the Center for Democracy and Technology.

The 1986 Electronic Communications Act gives people in the United States some protection from government interference of their e-mail. However, nothing protects people from the government viewing their Internet search history. Online companies keep Internet search logs. These logs show what people have searched for online. Companies such as Google can identify which users have visited which websites. People's search and browser histories are not specifically protected by any law.

In 2006, the U.S. government ordered Google to give it a sampling of Google's search logs. When Google refused, the government took Google to court, arguing that it needed the records to show that Internet filtering does not protect children from online pornography. The government stated it only wanted random samplings that could not be connected to individual people. On March 18, 2006, a federal judge ruled that Google had to give the government 50,000 random URLs people visited on the Internet. However, the court stated that the Department of Justice did not provide enough reason to force Google to give the government search terms entered by its users.

Privacy advocates said at the time that this incident was the start of a slippery slope—and it was. By 2014, the Justice Department asked the courts to grant it the ability to remotely access data stored electronically through computer searches. "It's one thing to say we're going to search a particular computer," said Chris Soghoian of the ACLU. "It's another thing to say we're going to search every computer that visits this website, without knowing how many there are going to be, without knowing what city, state or countries they're coming from."[51]

This would be, according to privacy advocates, a major invasion of privacy that could have serious consequences for individuals, even those who have done nothing wrong. For example, a researcher may look at websites that are propaganda for terrorists. Many who research terrorism, including the ACLU, have to read websites and magazines released by the terrorist group Islamic State of Iraq and Syria (ISIS) in order to understand what the group believes. Under restricted privacy rules, these researchers could end up on the government's terrorist watch list. This could cause them to be arrested or even jailed mistakenly.

In 2016, the FCC ruled that ISPs could not share or sell personal information, such as location or Internet history, without a consumer's permission. This privacy ruling restricted the use of personal data for business purposes. However, in 2017, Congress overturned that rule, so customers' data can now be shared with third parties without their knowledge or consent. Outraged citizens threatened to buy the private histories of Congress members who had voted to overturn the rule. However, the website The Verge clarified that this would be illegal under the Telecommunications Act, which "explicitly prohibits the sharing of 'individually identifiable' customer information except under very specific circumstances."[52] The law does allow the collection and sharing of aggregate data, which is data collected from multiple sources. Most people still consider this an invasion of privacy because ISPs are able to see a person's entire browsing history. Even though the ISP is not allowed to sell an individual's browsing history to a third party, it is still able to track the websites people visit and use that information themselves to target advertising to consumers.

Privacy and Law

Because there are so few clear-cut data privacy laws, U.S. courts have had to interpret current laws to deal with technology and privacy. Many of these rulings have been in favor of privacy. In 2007, a New Jersey appellate court ruled that computer users could expect that the personal information they give their ISPs to be considered private. The case indicates that some states are providing more privacy protection to computer users.

A law signed in 1998 by President Bill Clinton included a "Safe Harbor" provision for Internet traffic with the European Union. This allowed ISPs to transfer information from country to country. An Irish citizen brought a case against the Safe Harbor law. He had used Facebook since 2008. Facebook transfers data on its customers from their home country to its headquarters in the United States. The Irish citizen believed that in the wake of the exposure of the NSA's data collection by Edward Snowden, the United States could not provide for the safety of his personal information. The European Court of Justice agreed. It declared that the privacy of information is a fundamental right.

Privacy for Teen Reproductive Choices

Reproductive choices are a major privacy issue among teenagers. One issue is whether a teenager can get birth control pills without her parent's permission. In this case, most U.S. state laws protect teens' privacy. They can go to a health professional for birth control; however, some states require teens to get a parent's consent. Abortion is another hot topic. Many states have, or are considering, laws that require parent notification when a teenager decides to get an abortion. Opponents of notification laws believe these laws violate privacy. They also believe these laws force teens to get unsafe abortions. Supporters of notification laws say that parents have a right to know about any sort of medical procedure their teenage children are undergoing. "A parent or guardian should be made aware that their child is going to undergo any medical procedure," said Chris Kise, former state solicitor general in Florida. "Children in the public school system can't get an aspirin without parental notice and approval."[1] Almost all of the states that do have parental notification and consent laws also have judicial bypass options. These options allow a teen who feels she cannot involve her parents to get a judge's permission to proceed with her abortion.

1. Quoted in Lisa Greene, "Some Fear Effect of New Abortion Law," *St. Petersburg Times*, July 1, 2005. www.sptimes.com/2005/07/01/Tampabay/Some_fear_effect_of_a.shtml.

Privacy in Education

Children, like all people, are entitled to privacy rights, even at school. There are some laws that protect their rights while at school. The Family Educational Rights and Privacy Act (FERPA) protects the confidentiality of student educational records. All public schools as well as private schools that receive federal funding are covered by FERPA. The act gives students and their parents the right to inspect and review their own education records. They can also request corrections and stop the release of personally identifiable information.

Students have rights, but those rights are generally restricted in schools.

However, there are limits to student privacy. One controversial privacy issue involves searches of student cars and possessions. In the United States, the Fourth Amendment protects both adults and children and their property from unreasonable searches by the government. Unreasonable searches are those without search warrants. To get a search warrant, law enforcement officials must have probable cause that a crime was committed. It is different, however, in schools. A school official, such as a principal, does not need probable cause to search a backpack or purse. Judges have ruled that school officials have a right to keep control of what occurs at their school.

School officials have even more leeway when searching lockers. U.S. courts have found that lockers are shared property between the student and the school. This means the student should expect minimal privacy with his or her locker.

Drug and alcohol testing at school is another privacy issue. Some students believe testing is an invasion of their privacy. The U.S. Supreme Court has ruled that random drug testing is allowable when students participate in extracurricular activities. In the 2002 case *Board of Education v. Earls*, the Supreme Court held that all students who participate in voluntary activities, such as cheerleading, band, or debate, could be subjected to random tests. The Court reasoned that participating in these activities is a privilege, not a right.

Staying Informed

Although the United States has laws that protect people's civil liberties, individuals must sometimes fight to make sure those laws are upheld. They must also be informed about new laws being passed to make sure those laws do not violate the Constitution. Citizens have the right to protest any law they do not agree with; this practice helps keep the government accountable for its actions. Ignoring the government's actions allows officials to pass laws that may violate people's rights. Citizens are a key part of the democratic process and must make an effort to stay informed about what the government is doing regarding their civil liberties.

Chapter 1: The United States and Civil Liberties

1. David McCullough, *John Adams.* New York, NY: Simon & Schuster, 2001, p. 66.

2. Quoted from James Madison's speech in the Virginia Constitutional Convention, December 2, 1829. www.constitution.org/jm/18291202_vaconcon.txt.

3. "Do Noncitizens Have Constitutional Rights?," *Slate*, September 27, 2001. www.slate.com/articles/news_and_politics/explainer/2001/09/do_noncitizens_have_constitutional_rights.html.

4. "The Bill of Rights: A Brief History," American Civil Liberties Union, March 4, 2002. www.aclu.org/crimjustice/gen/10084res20020304.html.

5. "Modern History Sourcebook: Susan B. Anthony: Women's Right to Vote," Fordham University. sourcebooks.fordham.edu/mod/1873anthony.asp.

6. "The History Behind the Equal Rights Amendment," The Equal Rights Amendment. www.equalrightsamendment.org/history.htm.

Chapter 2: Freedom of Speech

7. Robert Shibley, "Cornell's Hostility to Free Speech Hits New Peak," FIRE, September 29, 2008. www.thefire.org/index.php/article/9738.html.

8. Quoted in "Constitution of the People's Republic of China," People's Daily Online, December 4, 1982. en.people.cn/constitution/constitution.html.

9. Quoted in Steven J. Heyman, *Hate Speech and the Constitution, Volume 2.* New York, NY: Garland Publishing, 1996, p. 165.

10. "Hate Speech on Campus," American Civil Liberties Union, 2017. www.aclu.org/other/hate-speech-campus?redirect=cp redirect/12808.

11. Chris Gauthier, "American Protests: Then and Now," *MCLA Beacon*, February 8, 2007. www.mclabeacon.com/media/storage/paper802/news/2007/02/08/Features/American.Protests.Then.And.Now-2704942.shtml.

12. Robin Seemangal, "Police Use Force Against Peaceful Protestors in DC," *Observer*, January 20, 2017. www.observer.com/2017/01/dc-police-trump-inauguration-protests-riots/.

13. "School Crime and Safety," National Institute of Justice, April 4, 2017. www.nij.gov/topics/crime/school-crime/pages/welcome.aspx.

14. "Banned Books in the United States," Adler and Robin Books. www.adlerbooks.com/banned.html.

15. Quoted in Claire Mullally, "Banned Books," First Amendment Center, September 29, 2008. www.firstamendmentcenter.org/speech/libraries/topic.aspx?topic=banned_books.

16 Shanna Lisberg, "5 Notable Banned-Book Cases for Banned Books Week," NWSidebar, September 26, 2014. nwsidebar.wsba.org/2014/09/26/banned-books-week/.

17. Mike Snider, Roger Yu, and Emily Brown, "What Is Net Neutrality and What Does It Mean for Me?," *USA Today*, February 24, 2015. www.usatoday.com/story/tech/2015/02/24/net-neutrality-what-is-it-guide/23237737/.

18. Vince Crawley, "Freedom's Watchdog: The Press in the United States," America.gov, June 1, 2008. www.america.gov/st/freepress-english/2008/June/20080601091649eaifas0.8963587.html.

Chapter 3: Freedom of Religion

19. "Chinese Government Accused of Burning Crosses in Christian Crackdown," CBS News, March 10, 2016. www.cbsnews.com/news/china-communist-party-crackdown-on-christians-religious-freedom/.

20. "China," International Coalition for Religious Freedom, May 9, 2004. www.religiousfreedom.com/wrpt/Chinarpt.htm.

21. "Religion in Public Schools," Anti-Defamation League, 2004. www.adl.org/religion_ps_2004/evolution.asp.

22. Associated Press, "New Jersey School Sued Over 'Under God' in Pledge," BigStory.com, April 22, 2014. bigstory.ap.org/

article/new-jersey-school-sued-over-under-god-pledge.

23. "A Teacher's Guide to Religion in the Public Schools," First Amendment Center. www.firstamendmentcenter.org/madison/wp-content/uploads/2011/03/teachersguide.pdf.

24. Barry Lynn, "Does Allowing Students to Cash In Their Vouchers at Schools with Religious Affiliation Violate the U.S. Constitution?," CNN, 2000. www.cnn.com/SPECIALS/2000/democracy/privateschools.publicmoney/views/index.html.

25. Quoted in "Court Backs Vouchers for Religious Schools," ABC News, June 27, 2002. abcnews.go.com/US/story?id= 91506.

26. "Religious Displays and the Courts," Pew Forum on Religion and Public Life, June 2007. pewforum.org/docs/?DocID=232.

Chapter 4: Civil Liberties and National Security

27. Abraham Lincoln, "Domestic Intelligence: A Proclamation," *Harper's Weekly*, October 11, 1862. www.sonofthesouth.net/leefoundation/civil-war/1862/october/lincoln-writ-habeas-corpus.htm.

28. Paul Burnett, "Red Scare," University of Missouri, Kansas City, Law School. www.law.umkc.edu/faculty/projects/ftrials/Sacco V/redscare.html.

29. Christopher Finan, *From the Palmer Raids to the Patriot Act*. Boston, MA: Beacon, 2007, p. 142.

30. Sheryl Gay Stolberg, "U.S. Senate Approves Revised Patriot Act," *New York Times*, March 3, 2006. www.nytimes.com/2006/03/03/world/americas/03iht-patriot.html.

31. Quoted in Dan Eggen, "Patriot Act Provisions Voided," *Washington Post*, September 27, 2007. www.washingtonpost.com/wp-dyn/content/article/2007/09/26/AR2007092602084.html.

32. Quoted in Eyder Peralta, "Parts of Patriot Act Expire, Even as Senate Moves on Bill Limiting Surveillance," NPR, May 31, 2015. www.npr.org/sections/thetwo-way/2015/05/31/411044789/live-blog-facing-midnight-deadline-the-senate-debates-parts-of-the-patriot-act.

33. Quoted in Anthony Lewis, "The Election and America's Future," *The New York Review of Books*, November 4, 2004. www.nybooks.com/articles/2004/11/04/the-election-and-americas-future/.

Chapter 5: Special Population Issues

34. Quoted in Stephen Ohlemacher, "Racial Disparities Persist Despite Election of First Black President," *Virginian-Pilot*, November 25, 2008, p. 3.

35. Quoted in Eric Nalder, Lewis Kamb, and Daniel Lathrop, "Blacks Are Arrested on 'Contempt of Cop' Charge at Higher Rate," *Seattle PI*, February 28, 2008. seattlepi.nwsource.com/local/353020_obstructmain28.asp.

36. Quoted in Ariane De Vogue, "Justice Sonia Sotomayor: Affirmative Action 'Opened Doors in My Life,'" ABC News, April 22, 2014. abcnews.go.com/blogs/politics/2014/04/justice-sonia-sotomayor-affirmative-action-opened-doors-in-my-life/.

37. Quoted in Cheryl Pellerin, "Carter Opens All Military Occupations, Positions to Women," U.S. Department of Defense, December 3, 2015. www.defense.gov/News/Article/Article/632536/carter-opens-all-military-occupations-positions-to-women.

38. Quoted in Jack Zahora, "Army Policies Don't Keep Women off Front Lines," NPR, August 26, 2007. www.npr.org/templates/story/story.php?storyId=13961298.

39. James Skillen, "Same-Sex 'Marriage' Is Not a Civil Right," Center for Public Justice, 2004. www.cpjustice.org/stories/storyReader$1178.

40. *Obergefell et al. v. Hodges*, Director, Ohio Department of Health, et al., 556 U.S. (2015). www.supremecourt.gov/opinions/14pdf/14-556_3204.pdf.

41. Kathy Belge, "Both Sides of the Issue," About.com. lesbianlife.about.com/cs/families/a/adoption_2.htm.

42. "Executive Order: Protecting the Nation from Foreign Terrorist Entry into the United States," the White House, January 27, 2017. www.whitehouse.gov/the-press-office/2017/01/27/executive-order-protecting-nation-foreign-terrorist-entry-united-states.

43. "Executive Order: Protecting the Nation from Foreign Terrorist Entry into the United States."

Chapter 6: A Right to Privacy

44. Quoted in "Supreme Court Strikes Down Texas Sodomy Law," CNN, November 18, 2003. www.cnn.com/2003/LAW/06/26/scotus.sodomy.

45. Quoted in Margaret Hartmann, "Brittany Maynard, 'Death With Dignity' Advocate, Ends Her Life," *New York*, November 3, 2014. nymag.com/daily/intelligencer/2014/11/death-with-dignity-backer-brittany-maynard-dies.html.

46. "Privacy Act of 1974," Electronic Privacy Information Center. epic.org/privacy/1974act.

47. Quoted in Rod Smith, "Casinos, Airlines Ordered to Give FBI Information," *Casino City Times*, December 31, 2003. www.casinocitytimes.com/news/article.cfm?contentID=140114.

48. David H. Holtzman, *Privacy Lost*. San Francisco, CA: Josey-Bass, 2006, p. 187.

49. Joelle Tessler, "Privacy Erosion: A 'Net Loss,'" *Congressional Quarterly*, Fall 2006, p. 14.

50. Testimony of James X. Dempsey, Senior Staff Counsel Center for Democracy and Technology before the Senate Judiciary Committee, September 6, 2000. www.cdt.org/files/testimony/000906dempsey.shtml.

51. Quoted in Kevin Poulsen, "Visit the Wrong Website, and the FBI Could End Up in Your Computer," *Wired*, August 5, 2014. www.wired.com/2014/08/operation_torpedo/.

52. Russell Brandom, "You Can't Buy Congress' Web History—Stop Trying," The Verge, March 29, 2017. www.theverge.com/2017/3/29/15115382/buy-congress-web-history-gop-fake-internet-privacy.

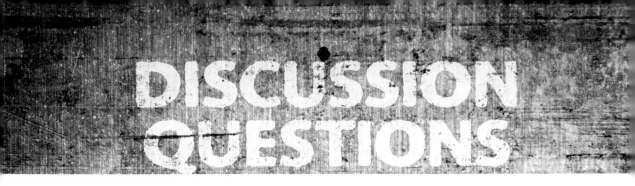

DISCUSSION QUESTIONS

Chapter 1: The United States and Civil Liberties

1. Why did James Madison believe the United States needed a bill of rights?

2. For years, many countries have violated women's property rights. Why are property rights so important?

3. What parallels can be drawn between the work of the ACLU and the UN? What different issues do they address?

Chapter 2: Freedom of Speech

1. Why do countries such as China restrict news agencies from criticizing the government on television, in newspapers, or on the Internet?

2. In the United States, why are "fighting words" against the law, and what makes them more than just offensive speech?

3. Why does the ACLU believe that all speech, even hate speech, should be protected by the First Amendment?

Chapter 3: Freedom of Religion

1. How do the Establishment and Free Exercise clauses of the First Amendment differ in their protection of religious freedom in the United States?

2. Why does the Communist government in China restrict religion?

3. After reading about the separation of church and state, do you agree that the Constitution allows for religious displays on government property? Why or why not?

Chapter 4: Civil Liberties and National Security

1. What are some examples of the U.S. government limiting civil liberties during times of war, and what were the government's reasons for doing so?

2. The Bush administration decided that al-Qaeda prisoners did not fall under the Geneva Conventions. What are some of the rights the prisoners were denied?

3. How has Congress addressed updating the Patriot Act, and why were some provisions changed?

Chapter 5: Special Population Issues

1. Why do opponents of racial profiling claim it is a violation of the Fourth Amendment?

2. What are the arguments for and against affirmative action?

3. Undocumented immigrants in the United States can only receive emergency care as of 2017. When might they need care outside of an emergency?

Chapter 6: A Right to Privacy

1. What are some issues in which one person's right to privacy might contradict another person's morals?

2. How does the European Court of Justice disagree with American privacy laws regarding the Internet?

3. When it comes to personal property, how does being on school grounds affect a student's right to privacy?

American Civil Liberties Union (ACLU)
125 Broad St., 18th Fl.
New York, NY 10004
(212) 549-2500
www.aclu.org
The ACLU is a nationwide organization with more than half a million members. Its mission is to guard the civil liberties of people in the United States. The ACLU works daily in courts, legislatures, and communities to defend people's rights and liberties guaranteed by the Constitution and the laws of the United States. Its website contains information about past and present court cases with which it is involved.

First Amendment Center/Newseum
555 Pennsylvania Ave.
Washington, D.C. 20001
(202) 292-6288
www.newseuminstitute.org/first-amendment-center
The First Amendment Center has an office at the Newseum Institute in Washington, D.C. The center coordinates with the Newseum staff to provide educational courses and speaking events.

James Madison Center
Wilson Hall, Rm. 205
MSC 1020
Harrisonburg, VA 22807
(540) 568-2549
www.jmu.edu/madison/center/home.htm
In 1999, the James Madison Center was founded in honor of the fourth U.S. president. The center holds information about Madison's life and times and about the Bill of Rights. It offers seminars, workshops, internships, and other professional opportunities for students, teachers, and members of the community. Information about Madison's reasons for proposing the Bill of Rights and its development can be found on the center's website.

National Association for the Advancement of Colored People (NAACP)
4805 Mt. Hope Dr.
Baltimore, MD 21215
(877) NAACP-98
www.naacp.org
The mission of the NAACP is to eliminate racial hatred and racial discrimination. It also works to protect the civil liberties of all persons through education, campaigns, and efforts to change laws. Its website provides updates on several civil liberties issues and describes how the NAACP is active in these issues.

National Organization of Women (NOW)
1100 H Street NW, Ste. 300
Washington, D.C. 20005
(202) 628-8669 (628-8NOW)
www.now.org
NOW is an organization of grassroots feminist activists with hundreds of chapters and hundreds of thousands of members and activists in all 50 states and the District of Columbia. Its goal is to bring about equality for all women. The organization works to eliminate discrimination and harassment in schools, the workplace, the justice system, and all other sectors of society. Its website contains information about ongoing women's issues and NOW's involvement in them.

Books

Berman, Ari. *Give Us the Ballot: The Modern Struggle for Voting Rights in America*. New York, NY: Farrar, Straus and Giroux, 2015.
This book discusses the 1965 Voting Rights Act, which gave all Americans the right to vote, and some of the challenges that Americans still face regarding this issue.

Darmer, Katherine B., Robert M. Baird, and Stuart E. Rosenbaum. *Civil Liberties vs. National Security in a Post 9/11 World*. Amherst, NY: Prometheus, 2004.
This title explores the effects 9/11 had on civil liberties in the United States.

Friedman, Ian. *Freedom of Speech and the Press*. New York, NY: Facts On File, 2005.
This title explores the beginnings of freedom of speech and the press in the United States. It also discusses current free expression issues.

Karson, Jill, ed. *Contemporary Issues: Civil Liberties*. Farmington Hills, MI: Greenhaven Press, 2006.
In this book, Karson explores the effects of terrorism on civil liberties, current free expression issues, and today's religious issues.

Merino, Noël. *Domestic Surveillance*. Farmington Hills, MI: Greenhaven Press, 2016.
This book discusses the conflicting opinions that arise when a government watches its citizens.

Pauly, Robert. *Speech, Media, and Protest*. Broomall, PA: Mason Crest, 2017.
Free speech and the right to protest are vital parts of democracy. Readers learn about how to take an active part in their government.

Websites

Findlaw.com
civilrights.findlaw.com/civil-rights-overview/civil-rights-vs-civil-liberties.html
This website helps to define civil liberties versus civil rights in the United States.

First Amendment Center
www.firstamendmentcenter.org
The First Amendment Center's website provides daily updates about First Amendment–related developments; detailed reports about U.S. Supreme Court cases involving the First Amendment; and commentary, analyses, and special reports involving free expression, press freedom, and religious freedom issues.

Privacy International (PI)
www.privacyinternational.org
PI is a human rights group that began in 1990. Its goal is to protect people from privacy invasions by governments and corporations. PI is based in London and works with partner organizations around the world on privacy issues. Its website has updates on its actions throughout the world and provides information about individual countries and their privacy situations.

Privacy Rights Clearinghouse
www.privacyrights.org
This website aims to inform people of their right to privacy online and to provide information on technology's effects on privacy.

United Nations Human Rights
www.ohchr.org
The mission of the UN Office of the High Commissioner for Human Rights is to protect human rights around the world. It does so by monitoring its member states to ensure that they are complying with international human rights treaties. It also promotes human rights through education and public information. Its website provides information on human rights efforts around the world.

INDEX

Cover wh1600/Getty Images; p. 6 MPI/Getty Images; p. 7 David Smart/Shutterstock.com; p. 10 Andrii Bielov/Shutterstock.com; pp. 12, 16 courtesy of the Library of Congress; p. 13 courtesy of the National Archives; pp. 18, 50 Everett Historical/Shutterstock.com; p. 20 Bettmann/Contributor/Getty Images; p. 24 Radoslaw Lecyk/Shutterstock.com; p. 30 Ethan Miller/Getty Images; p. 32 Andrew Burton/Getty Images; p. 34 Monkey Business Images/Monkey Business/Thinkstock; p. 36 Lawrey/Shutterstock.com; p. 39 PHILIPPE LOPEZ/AFP/Getty Images; p. 40 Kzenon/Shutterstock.com; p. 44 FatCamera/E+/Getty Images; pp. 47, 74 Alex Wong/Getty Images; p. 51 AFP PHOTO/AFP/Getty Images; p. 52 IM_VISUALS/Shutterstock.com; p. 57 The Guardian via Getty Images; pp. 60, 62 John Moore/Getty Images; p. 65 Allison Joyce/Getty Images; p. 67 Tom Williams/CQ Roll Call/Getty Images; pp. 69 TONY KARUMBA/AFP/Getty Images; p. 72 Jessica McGowan/Getty Images; p. 79 corgarashu/Shutterstock.com; p. 84 Den Rise/Shutterstock.com; p. 86 Monkey Business Images/Shutterstock.com; p. 90 AP Photo/The Mountain Press, Curt Habraken.

ABOUT THE AUTHOR

Allison Krumsiek is an author and poet living in Washington, D.C. When she isn't writing or editing, she can be found fearlessly defending civil liberties.

31901062563145